# YOU WERE BORN

# MORE

# YOU WERE BORN

## *for*

# MORE

*Six Steps to Breaking Through to Your Destiny*

## HARRY R. JACKSON JR.

### Chosen

*a division of Baker Publishing Group*
Minneapolis, Minnesota

© 2013 by Harry R. Jackson, Jr.

Published by Chosen Books
11400 Hampshire Avenue South
Bloomington, Minnesota 55438
www.chosenbooks.com

Chosen Books is a division of
Baker Publishing Group, Grand Rapids, Michigan

Printed in the United States of America

Library of Congress Cataloging-in-Publication Data
Jackson, Harry R.
    You were born for more : six steps to breaking through to your destiny / Harry R. Jackson, Jr.
        pages cm
    Summary: "Discover the six unfailing steps to life-transforming breakthrough and restoration. They will help you experience God's favor, rise above your circumstances, and achieve lasting change"—Provided by publisher.
    ISBN 978-0-8007-9556-6 (pbk. : alk. paper)
    1. Change (Psychology)—Religious aspects—Christianity. 2. Success—Religious aspects—Christianity. 3. Christian life. I. Title.
BV4599.5.C44J33 2013
248.4—dc23                                                        2013002989

Cover design by Kirk DouPonce, DogEared Design

13   14   15   16   17   18   19        7   6   5   4   3   2   1

This book is dedicated to my two daughters,
J. Michele Jackson and Elizabeth R. Jackson,
without whose love, faith and support
my wife, Vivian,* and I could never
have survived our darkest years of crisis.
May the things you sowed into our lives
be repaid a hundred times over!


Agape, Harry and Vivian Jackson

* Please see footnote on page 190.

# CONTENTS

# ACKNOWLEDGMENTS

his book is a story of a powerful journey I have taken over the past seven years. Without my wife, Vivian, I never would have been able to complete the journey. She is truly inspiration personified.

My beloved daughters, J. Michele and Elizabeth, and my mother, Essie, have also spent countless hours and unbounded energy seeing to my needs, physically, emotionally and mentally. This care gave me the capacity to hear from the Holy Spirit and learn the lessons that I have shared in this volume.

Jim Nelson Black has painstakingly put feet to the sermons that bore the principles contained in these pages. Thanks to his vision and strategic writing gift, I was able to extract precious nuggets of truth and to present them clearly for our readers. He also has a spirit of excellence that enhances the concepts and stories through this work.

Jane Campbell has always been an encouragement to me. She was one of the first people to discern that my ministry team and

I had valuable things to share with the Body of Christ through the written word. Without her encouragement, I would have never been able to focus time, energy and resources we have on our writing projects.

I appreciate Jeff Braun, our editor on this project. He brought a wealth of theological content, perspective and professionalism to the book development process. There are too many others at Chosen Books, including Carra Carr and the entire marketing and sales team, who are a wonderful group of people.

I appreciate Jan Sherman and her being involved in all the writing projects over the years. Nonetheless, the caliber of the work on this project has passed anything we have done before. Without her input and project management, I could not have pulled all the elements of this project together.

Most of all, thank You, Father, for this opportunity to share my understanding of Your love, grace and faithfulness. May this project and our ministry bring glory to Your name for many years to come.

# INTRODUCTION

*The Promise of Transforming Grace*

*H*as it happened to you? In the darkest hours of life, have you come face-to-face with your greatest need? Maybe you looked in the mirror one morning and saw someone you no longer recognized, or someone you no longer wanted to be. Maybe you have struggled with the loss of a loved one, a spouse, a dear friend or a relationship that somehow went wrong. Or maybe, like me, you have heard the sobering words from a doctor telling you, "The diagnosis is not good." In these and similar situations, there is hope. But in every case, our greatest need is for someone to rescue us.

When accidents happen, when illness strikes or when the rent comes due and things are completely out of control, what we need is someone to walk beside us and keep us from stumbling. But no earthly friend can, in and of themselves, be the solo go-to person. In my darkest moments, Jesus, my Lord and Savior, has become the friend that "sticketh closer than a brother." He is there beside me, encouraging me and holding me up.

Unfortunately, there are times when I do not feel God's presence. My prayers go unanswered and the whole world seems oblivious to my pain. Suddenly I feel alone, so I cry out. Jesus Himself quoted a prophetic psalm as He was dying on the cross: "My God, my God, why hast thou forsaken me?" (Psalm 22:1; Matthew 27:46; Mark 15:34 KJV). The truth is, I am never alone. God has not moved. He is always there, even in the most stressful and difficult times, but for some reason the phone feels off the hook, as if I am unreachable.

The situation is all too familiar, isn't it? To complicate things, we sometimes create barriers between ourselves and the Lord. We know that David sinned with Bathsheba and made other serious mistakes. David's sins, like ours, were internally complicated. Yes, lust and presumption were involved with Bathsheba. But in those days it was common for a king to take in the family of a fallen general. Marrying the widow would have been seen as an act of kindness. Still, after the sin of adultery, David made things even worse by getting Uriah killed on the battlefield. David's desire was to save face, to hide his sin. We often fall into the same trap by rationalizing and excusing ourselves from sin. We attempt to put perfume on the corpse of wrong motives or we attempt to dress up bad actions in the graveclothes of rationalization, in the name of positive thinking.

In the midst of trials, when we are hurting and cry out in desperation, God is always faithful. But He is also watching to see how we respond to His guidance and correction. David was punished repeatedly for his sins, stripped bare of his excuses. But against this backdrop, he never completely turned away from God again. Instead, he grew in his knowledge of God. In my book *The Way of the Warrior* (Chosen), I explore David's life journey in detail. As he expressed in the Twenty-third Psalm, the Lord's rod and his staff comforted him. The shepherd would use his rod as an instrument of correction with the sheep, the staff as an instrument of intervention to keep the sheep on the right path.

It is reassuring to know that the great saints of the Bible were human, too, and struggled with trials and tribulations, just as we do. When a personal crisis hits us, we can, through the grace of God, get back to basics and begin to rebuild our foundation. Our goal must always be to reconnect with Him through prayer, praise and His written Word. We must remind ourselves of His promise to never leave us or forsake us. In fact, early in my salvation experience, I memorized two powerful verses:

- He that cometh to God must believe that he is, and that he is a rewarder of them that diligently seek him. (Hebrews 11:6 KJV)
- Him that cometh to me I will in no wise cast out. (John 6:37 KJV)

So, how do we come to God?

## Finding Your Power Source

Sooner or later we all get to a place in our lives where we have no other recourse but to rely on God's supernatural grace. We cannot jump over life's hurdles anymore without a boost. We have got to get back up and start running. But to take the next step—to move beyond our weakness, our fears and our limitations—we have got to make changes, and that requires a power greater than our own.

What needs to change in your life? It may be a financial situation, problems with a personal relationship, a child who won't listen to reason anymore, or maybe it is the general direction your life is going. Some of us are facing physical issues that are genuinely life threatening. Others have been snared by the desire for riches and personal comfort to the extent that they are becoming narcissistic in their approach to God's grace. They start thinking *It's all about me!* and drift from the Word of God toward the phantoms of self-indulgence and self-gratification. No wonder the phone is off the hook.

Sometimes we can be our own worst enemy. We come to believe the world revolves around us instead of our lives revolving around God. If we are not getting everything we think we are entitled to, we can easily fall prey to a victim mentality, which is always followed by defeat and discouragement. What we need to understand is that God has a plan for our lives. He wants to lavish His favor upon us, but we can only experience the transforming power of God's love by cooperating with His sovereign grace. If you truly want to see your world transformed, you must get out of yourself and get back to your power source: Jesus.

This book is about grace, one of the most fundamental aspects of the Christian faith. I wish I could give you an explanation of grace in lofty theological terms, but I don't have the space to tackle that job here. The writings of Charles Spurgeon, Charles Ryrie, David Jeremiah and Max Lucado can do that. My work here is an attempt to take this lofty theological term and make *grace* accessible in our seasons of crises. As I have experienced, grace is a divine force that meets us, transforms us and leads us into God's purpose and destiny.

> *We can only experience the transforming power of God's love by cooperating with His sovereign grace.*

I want to harmonize with the words of Paul, who said, "I do not frustrate the grace of God" (Galatians 2:21 KJV). I also want to help you discern the "time of your visitation" (Luke 19:41–44) instead of facing rebuke by Jesus for missing your moment or hiding your talents (see Matthew 25:14–28). As I said, I want to help you plug back in to our power source.

That is what I am talking about. Real and lasting change is more than simply developing a positive attitude or taking a few steps of action based on a psychological grid. It means stopping right where you are and reevaluating what you have been working for. It means finding a pathway back to the true source of strength in your life. It means turning around and going back to where you know you belong.

That is what the word *repentance* actually means. The original New Testament word is *metanoia*, meaning to change your mind and go a different way. When you finally come to your senses and realize that nothing you are doing is giving you the results you want, you need to stop right where you are and turn around. That is the first step. Yes, you may need to get down on your knees and repent—you know what I mean—but to get the phone service back up and restore communications with the One who can actually help get you back on track, you have got to settle up with the phone company and get the power back on. This process is not negative; it leads us down a godly path that lifts us out of the control of the flesh (see Galatians 5:17–26). There have been a lot of imbalanced teachings on grace that try to minimize a believer's need to ask God's forgiveness of sin and to turn one's life around. These teachings just throw Scriptures like 1 John 1:7–10 into the trash bin:

> But if we walk in the light, as he is in the light, we have fellowship with one another, and the blood of Jesus, his Son, purifies us from all sin. If we claim to be without sin, we deceive ourselves and the truth is not in us. If we confess our sins, he is faithful and just and will forgive us our sins and purify us from all unrighteousness. If we claim we have not sinned, we make him out to be a liar and his word has no place in our lives.
>
> *NIV1984*

In this passage, God promises to forgive us of personal sin and to walk us through a process of untwisting and healing the broken areas in our character and inner life before Him. This transformation of forgiveness, healing and restoration of character makes way for deep personal joy.

If you have never experienced the restoration of your character through repentance, I want to pause and invite you to pray a prayer with me. This prayer is simple, but when you have spoken it with a sincere heart, the results are eternal. Let's pray:

*Lord Jesus, I need You. Thank You for dying on the cross for my sins. I open the door of my life and receive You as my Savior and Lord. Thank You for forgiving me of my sins and giving me eternal life. Take control of the throne of my life. Make me the kind of person You want me to be. Amen.*

Welcome to the family of God! If you would like receive further instruction in your faith, please contact us at hopeinfo @thehopeconnection.org.

Peter says in the New Testament that this walk is "joy unspeakable and full of glory" (1 Peter 1:8 KJV). Joy is what Jesus promises us! Internal peace and powerful joy released through prayer and praise should be stabilizing factors in all of our lives. We are not alone! He walks with us! But like the psalmist declares to Asaph and to us, we must acknowledge our personal failings and sins (see Psalm 50). Unfortunately, many today are preaching the gospel of accommodation instead of the gospel of transformation.

## Partners on the Journey

In this book I am proposing a pathway to restoration and transformation that has been proven to work time and time again. It has worked for me and countless others. We are all partners on this journey, and it begins with recommitting your life to Jesus Christ, who is the source of transformation you have been looking for. Without that important first step, the effort will be futile. Second, it means reconnecting with the interactive power of God's grace through faith. And, third, it means living in such a way that, each and every day, you are a beacon to those around you, reflecting the light of God's love in the world.

This book is about "Step Two" of this process—connecting with the interactive power of God. You are going to learn how to stabilize yourself in a crisis and then embrace four dimensions of grace:

1. Survival grace (divine providence; see Hebrews 1:2–3)

2. Visionary grace (the Spirit-filled life; see Acts 1:1–9)

3. Transitional grace (entering into supernatural covenant with God around your calling; see Leviticus 2:13; 2 Chronicles 13:5)

4. Establishment grace (pursuing personal holiness; see 1 Corinthians 1:2)

Do not worry about these irreligious terms. Giving you a practical paradigm for breakthrough and success is my goal here.

I have been privileged to share aspects of my own journey many times in previous books as well as on television and radio and in my sermons at Hope Christian Church. I have been the beneficiary of God's favor more times than I can count, resting in His strength through times of trial and temptation, through battles with cancer, as well as the strains of a very busy schedule. In all these things, I have been tested and come close to the limits of my endurance. But in the nick of time I have gained renewed strength and confidence by the transforming power of grace, and that is a big part of the story I want to share in these pages.

I want you to experience the favor of God. I want you to feel the peace and joy that come from knowing you are on the right track. I want you to know that with God's help, you can transform your world, no matter what your situation is today. God has promised to give you the desires of your heart, but your motives must be pure and your heart

> *The power to break through your problems and enter into realms of blessing is within reach.*

must be accessible to His guidance to receive the blessing. The power to break through your problems and enter into realms of blessing is within reach, but it requires an open and honest relationship between you and God. The great Christian reformers had this power. Your grandparents who were the prayer warriors and saints of former generations had it as well. So what is holding you back?

## Channels of Blessing

Part of the problem is that we live in a hardhearted secular age that has turned away from God and fallen in love with personal pleasure. For some folks, their first love is apparently technology. Instead of trusting in the Redeemer of mankind, they put their trust in iPods and smartphones and all the expensive fads and fantasies that everyone is so taken with.

21

With all the gizmos and gadgets we have accumulated, it would be easy to get the idea that we are smarter or more sophisticated than the men and women of other times. We start to look down on our parents and grandparents, and some of our young folks have convinced themselves the Christian life is old-fashioned and meaningless, but that is such a dangerous gamble.

Sadly, many Christians have been seduced by the false glamour of the popular culture. We would rather be thought of as trendy and cool than as obedient followers of Jesus Christ. Turning our backs on the glitter of this world is just too big a leap. Making the kinds of character and lifestyle choices we would need to make in order to receive the blessings of God is an obstacle, so we turn our backs on God and miss out on the blessings we might have had.

That is why the power is off. That is why the phone lines have gone dead. Our dot-com generation needs to hear this message most of all, because our plugged-in lifestyles have so many of us thinking we have everything we need. But do not be fooled. It is only a matter of time until all those electronic gadgets will be junk, out of date, replaced by some other gadgets. The issues we face will still be there, and if the pleasures and playthings of this world are all we have to believe in, we will be just as empty as we were before. Any of us who gets the idea we have outgrown our need for God is in for a rude awakening.

The promise of transforming grace comes to us in specific ways, with specific purposes and specific requirements. But until we learn to embrace the transformation that only Jesus

Christ can offer, the door to spiritual blessings must remain closed. Refusing to turn away from sin and self-deception is a deal breaker with God, barring us from the breakthrough that Christ desires for each of us.

On the other hand, choosing to live an empowered life, transformed by the grace of God and the discipleship of godly teachers and mentors, will bring us into the kind of relationship with God that opens up channels of blessing and opportunity like nothing else in this world. That is what this book is about.

# — 1 —

# THE PATHWAY
# TO BLESSINGS

### Step One: Have a Humble
### and Willing Spirit

*I*t was my birthday, February 4, 2006, and I found myself waking up in the intensive care unit of the world-famous Johns Hopkins Hospital in Baltimore with a pleasant but stern nurse hovering over me. Peering into my eyes, she informed me I had been asleep for over twelve hours. I soon learned that the seven and a half hour surgery to remove a cancerous golf-ball-sized tumor and most of my esophagus had been successful.

The problem was that I was still in intensive care. An emergency procedure was necessary to prevent blood clots from circulating through my body. I also had a severe case of heart arrhythmia. In other words, my heartbeat was unstable. It would descend at times as low as 80 beats per minute and then suddenly shoot up to as high as 180 beats per minute without warning.

This was a major concern for the physicians because I had already had a stroke and another near-fatal incident during the initial phase of my treatment. My doctor said that most people in my condition had only a 10 percent chance of survival. If I made it through this procedure successfully, however, the odds would increase to a 60 percent chance of survival.

For this reason, the doctors had waited for weeks to set up the surgery. They were afraid I would expire on the operating table if my system did not somehow stabilize itself before the surgery. On the other hand, if we waited too long the cancer would metastasize and spread throughout my body. From a human perspective, it was as if fate had chosen this date as my last chance at life and deliverance. God, however, had a different idea.

Later that morning I saw an article in the early edition of Sunday's *Baltimore Sun*. It was a lengthy piece headlined "Seizing the Moral Mantle," with the subhead, "Q&A with Bishop Harry R Jackson Jr.: Influential minister's agenda for black America blends conservative and liberal positions." As the article pointed out, I had experienced a meteoric rise from relative obscurity to national prominence over the previous fifteen months. In all things relating to the church, particularly in regard to politics and race relations, I had suddenly become a voice. Many people had commented on all the media attention I was getting. Now here in the pages of the *Baltimore Sun* was confirmation that my voice was being heard.

A book I coauthored in 2004 with researcher, consultant and church growth expert Dr. George Barna, *High Impact African-American Churches*, had seemingly given me a greater level of authority. The book was based on ten years of research focusing on over four hundred black churches, their leaders and their members. Ironically, the book was not widely read by the general population, but the research was important, and perhaps the most surprising result of the book was that it helped to launch me into an expanded public role, offering commentary about current events on secular media outlets.

The newspaper article was a tremendous encouragement to my entire family, but it also confirmed to the doctors and nurses in America's number-one hospital that I was actually a celebrity. The surgeon even joked that they had Googled my name during the hours-long, start-and-stop procedure. They told me they were impressed, but I remembered that the great English pastor and author Charles Haddon Spurgeon, known as "the prince of preachers," often referred to celebrity as an example of God's grace. Pastors and teachers are not lifted up for their own sake, he believed, but so the beacon of God's love could shine forth through them. He wrote an entire book on the subject, in fact, entitled *Grace: God's Unmerited Favor*.

> *The truth is, I was just an emaciated black cancer patient in a city of considerable racial strife.*

To my mind, celebrity is almost a laughable concept, especially since my biblically based views on politics and popular culture have exposed me to a great deal of persecution over the years. Nevertheless, I have accepted the opportunities public attention has given me—in this case, better care from my doctors and nurses. The truth is, I was just an emaciated black cancer patient in a city of considerable racial strife. I simply needed expert care not often available at regional hospitals. In every other way I was just like the hundreds of people I had seen marching in and out of Johns Hopkins over the previous six months.

## God's Healing Grace

Many days it seemed as if my fellow patients were on a spiritual pilgrimage. They were not headed to a place of worship such as Jerusalem or Mecca, however. Their pilgrimage was more like visiting one of those sacred shrines you see on TV where people go to experience visions, healings and miracles. They go there with the expectation they will have an encounter with God. In some ways they were like the crippled man Jesus healed at the pool of Bethesda as he was waiting for an angel to stir the waters (see John 5:1–15).

Many of the men and women I saw each day were desperate but hopeful. I will never forget the little man who sat in a wheelchair with only his torso and arms remaining. His skin was the color of pale green pea soup. He often grimaced in pain as he waited for the various treatments he was undergoing at the Weinberg Cancer Center. His faithful wife wheeled him everywhere he needed to go, waiting attentively, never complaining. Her pilgrimage was not somber or morbid. Her journey was filled with the hope that the brilliant doctors at the nation's foremost teaching hospital would do the impossible once again and restore her husband to a dimension of health.

The difference between these other patients and myself was simple. I expected the best from medicine but also believed in a higher authority than those gifted doctors. God would decide whether I lived or died. At the beginning, however, I did not know my role in the miracle I desired. I did not know exactly whether I should be passive or active. After all, some theologians argue that healing is a covenant right. Others are adamant that the days of healing and miracles are past, but they pray to God to touch them in times of trouble.

After a few days of facing a death sentence for a diagnosis (less than 10 to 15 percent chance of my survival), I told my oldest daughter I would win no matter what happened. If what I preached was true, death would bring me into the Lord's presence (a win!). And if God healed me, I would go forth with a renewed sense of mission in my life (a win!). Suddenly Job 13:15 made sense to me: "Though he slay me, yet will I trust in him" (KJV). I had entered into a place of rest. No, I had not given up, but I realized more than ever that I could trust God. Shortly after that conversation with my daughter, I knew I was to aggressively pursue medical treatment, while understanding that my trust was really in the name of the Lord (see Psalm 20:7).

I wept and thanked God for the encouragement I had gotten from the newspaper article. I thought to myself, *If God had given up on the prospects of my healing, He would not have gone to the trouble of sending me such an encouraging message.* I could not help thinking that the newspaper article and accompanying picture of me was a personal birthday gift. As strange as the idea may sound to some folks, I relish the knowledge that I serve a God who knows me by name!

Yes, there are times when God can seem distant and out of touch, but we should be encouraged knowing we have a God who has chosen to reach out to us, so that those who truly love Him may experience the joy of knowing Him personally.

God's nature is shown throughout the Old Testament by His covenant name, Jehovah (or Yahweh). Most scholars believe that Yahweh is the only personal name that Israel had for God. Other names were simply descriptive phrases or titles. Yahweh was the name of God revealed to Moses on Mount Horeb. The name literally means "the revealing one." I am convinced the more we grow in our relationship with Him, the more God reveals Himself to us. As we see in Exodus 3:7, God let Moses know He was sending him to Egypt because He had seen the afflictions of His people. Because of His unfailing love for His chosen ones who were suffering in bondage, He transferred to Moses both an understanding of the plight of His people and a deep sense of compassion for them.

*The heart of God is a heart of compassion.*

That was something I needed to understand as I lay there in my hospital bed—that the heart of God is a heart of compassion. And over those ten long and trying days, I was confident that Jehovah God would never leave me or forsake me, as He promised in Deuteronomy 31:8 and Hebrews 13:5. Later that day my birthday ended with a dramatic prayer, which I offered to God in joined hands with my mother and my oldest daughter. As three generations of Jacksons were praying, the heart monitor rang out with a series of annoying beeps and a bright red digital reading, signaling a steady rise of 100, 120, 130, 140 and up to 180 beats per minute.

In a situation like that, facing the prospect of imminent demise, some people would have been tempted to start digging around in the cobwebs of their memories for evidence of unrepented sin. We live in a world today that always wants to play both ends against the middle. We want to live on the edge and have the best of both worlds, and when a crisis hits, we feverishly work to "clean up." Not me! I already had prayed and repented for incidents, attitudes, ill-spoken words and other regrettable mistakes going back decades. I had made peace with God. So as we watched that machine at my bedside, threatening and warning me of my all-too-human weakness, I was resolved to stand strong in my faith.

During the six months of treatments leading up to surgery, I had experienced a stroke that paralyzed my entire right side. I also was unable to speak during that incident. My speech and the use of my right hand and leg returned after several hours of tentative silence. The stroke had been induced by the intense treatment schedule. First, I had been given a hip pack that pumped chemo directly into my body every two minutes or so. Next, I received a three- to four-hour chemo treatment every seven to ten days at the hospital. Third, I received radiation treatment five days a week for over five weeks. These treatments made it difficult for me to eat food or even drink water.

My body did not respond well to these traumatic treatments. I had to have a liquid diet pumped into my lower intestines through a feeding tube during this critical period. I had come through so many problems and so many hurdles that I was sure of two things: (1) The Lord had given me a personal promise of healing in His Scriptures and (2) the newspaper article I had read was indeed a personal birthday card from God!

The Holy Spirit sent a renewed sense of peace and strength into my body, and what flooded my spirit while we prayed was not fear but the boldness of faith—a faith not riddled with the spiritual cancer of doubt that could block the free flow of God's healing power.

## Renewal and Resolve

After experiencing so many powerful emotions, I was finally at peace with the process. Surrounded by my family, I prayed the words of Jesus from Psalm 31:5 and Luke 23:46: "Father, into your hands I commit My spirit." After that prayer of commitment, my heart monitor began to descend slowly and I lay back on my bed exhausted. When I awoke the next morning, I felt wonderful and the arrhythmia never returned.

What were the chances that a major newspaper would write such a positive article about me at such a strategic time—an article that accurately articulated my understanding of God's calling on my life at that time? When I reread the story a few days later, I was inspired again. Like Eric Liddell, the amazing Christian athlete who competed and won a gold medal in the 1924 Olympics, I believed God had a purpose for my life, and the article was a confirmation of that fact.

In the Oscar-winning movie about his achievement, *Chariots of Fire*, Eric Liddell expressed the feelings much better than I could have done, but I knew what he meant. When his sister confronted him, concerned that Eric was putting athletic competition ahead of his calling to the mission field, he responded, "I believe that God made me for a purpose, but he also made me fast. When I run, I feel his pleasure."

In my case, I could almost hear the voice of God saying, "Run, Harry, run!" At that point I knew that I would live and not die. My prayer to commit my spirit into God's hands was not only what Christ had prayed on the cross, it was a prayer offered nightly by every Hebrew child during the days of Jesus' growing up. It had the same heartfelt sentiment as the first prayer my mother taught me:

> Now I lay me down to sleep,
> I pray the Lord my soul to keep.
> If I should die before I wake,
> I pray the Lord my soul to take.

It does not take much imagination or courage to react with anger when things are not going your way. When times are tough, when illness strikes or when the bill collectors come calling and the money is running out, it is easy to play the victim. But that only makes things worse. The secret is to place all your cares at the foot of the cross, knowing that the

God who loves you with an everlasting love has promised to guide your footsteps and give you the courage to overcome those challenges.

Looking back at all the remarkable things God has done in my life, I believe there are six practical steps that every child of God can take to radically transform their lives, their relationships, their happiness and their ultimate destiny. Once you commit your life to Jesus Christ, the first step is to connect with the interactive power of divine grace through the daily practice of humility. The American culture does not value humility. The humility I am speaking of comes in three dimensions of interrelated or variegated hues:

The fear of the Lord

Meekness

Radical obedience

The fear of the Lord is mentioned over and over again in the Bible (25 times in the New American Standard version). It is described specifically as the beginning of wisdom and a key to developing understanding and practical application of the Word of God (see Psalm 111:10). It brings a sense of cheer and inner joy, according to Proverbs 14:27; it is a fountain of life and leads to life (see Proverbs 14:27; 19:23). Finally, when teamed with humility it brings riches, honor and life (see Proverbs 22:4).

The fear of the Lord could be defined as the reverential awe of God. This attitude of extreme honor and allegiance to God has begun to give me a great reverence for both Scripture reading and personal worship.

The fear of the Lord is expressed very well in a worship chorus I learned years ago:

> I admire You
> I'm fascinated by You, Lord
> One thing have I desired, Lord
> Is to love You more and more
>
> For Your love is beyond compare
> And there is none like You—anywhere
> It's not that I loved You, but that You loved me
>    first
> And it's for Your wonderful, wonderful love that
>    I thirst
>
>                                        Unknown

In order to take the commands of Scripture seriously, we should choose to read the Scriptures as a message from the only One who deserves our highest adoration and our highest fear of judgment or wrath. He, after all, can reward us with heaven or hell and everything in between. Nonetheless, He loves us.

The second aspect of humility comes from the biblical concept of meekness. I debated whether I should share this with you at this time, but it will give you a picture of the understanding I developed early in my journey from both physical and emotional sickness to health.

*Baker's Bible Dictionary* reminded me that, although the ancient Near East culture placed a high value on meekness, our Western culture does not hold the concept in high regard. To be meek seems like you are being weak. Most modern translations of the Bible replace the noun *meekness* with *gentleness* or *humility* because our culture does not understand it.

Numbers 12:3 describes Moses as the most humble man on the face of the earth. In Matthew 11:29 Jesus says, "Take my yoke upon you and learn from me, for I am gentle and humble in heart, and *you will find rest for your souls*" (NIV, emphasis mine).

Yes, you have already figured it out. The words translated here as "humble" and "gentle" should have been translated as "meek." Moses was the meekest man on the face of the earth, and Jesus invited the burdened to come receive His yoke and mantle of service. The meekness described in both of these passages is best understood as surrender to God. On the surface, the discipline and self-control to bear up under difficult circumstances may look like the whipped puppy dog expression that comes from folks who have lost their dignity and their hope. Meekness, however, is a choice anchored in strength. Meekness endures hardship for a reason, and it attracts the grace of God.

William Barclay, the great Scottish theologian of the last century, gave a detailed explanation of the three distinctively different nuances in meaning of the original Greek word *meekness* by examining Matthew 5:5. The verse we know as "Blessed are the meek, for they shall inherit the earth" could also be translated in these ways:

1. "Blessed are those who are always angry at the right time, and never angry at the wrong time," for they shall inherit the earth.

2. "Blessed are . . . those who are completely *God*-controlled, for only in his service do we find our perfect freedom and, in doing his will, our peace," for they shall inherit the earth.

3. "Blessed are those who have the humility to know their own ignorance, their own weakness, and their own need," for they shall inherit the earth.[1]

If we attempt to become more humble without being meek, it is like drinking water without the wet or drinking Pepsi Cola without the bubbles and fizz. True humility involves a dimension of voluntary meekness that controls our human anger, surrenders to God's control and maintains the attitude of a learner.

Finally, humility involves a commitment to radical obedience. This third dimensional building block of humility is the natural final step that follows reverential fear of God and meekness. The things we become convinced are the will of God for our lives, we must pursue with intensity. Proverbs 28:1 says, "The wicked flee when no man pursueth: but the righteous are bold as a lion."

The apostle Peter says it this way: "Therefore humble yourselves under the mighty hand of God, that He may exalt you in due time, casting all your care upon Him, for He cares for you" (1 Peter 5:6–7). Building your relationship with God demands trust and a humble and willing spirit. But there are two things you must have in order to approach God in this way.

First, you must come to Him openly and honestly. You cannot hold out on God; you have to empty your spiritual

---

1. William Barclay, *New Testament Words*, rev. up. ed. (Westminster John Knox Press: Louisville, Ky.: 2001), 111–113.

pockets of everything you have been holding back—habits, doubts, fears, dirty little secrets. You must recognize Jesus Christ as the Son of God, as your Savior and the Lord of your life, if you want to receive His favor. And after you have repented and asked for forgiveness, you must be willing to make the changes in your attitudes, language and lifestyle that the Holy Spirit reveals to you, regardless of how difficult it is.

If you were invited to come to the White House to meet the president, I am pretty sure you would get yourself all cleaned up and put on your best suit. You would look your best and be on your best behavior out of respect for the office of the president. I am sure you would be proud to be there—an invitation would be an honor—and you would be humble in that place, wouldn't you?

Let me tell you something: The Son of God is infinitely greater and more important than all the presidents and kings and potentates who have ever lived, and God says you must be humble in His presence.

> God also has highly exalted Him and given Him the name which is above every name, that at the name of Jesus every knee should bow, of those in heaven, and of those on earth, and of those under the earth, and that every tongue should confess that Jesus Christ is Lord, to the glory of God the Father.
>
> *Philippians 2:9–11*

Everyone will bow before Him—both believers and nonbelievers—and only those who have been saved by grace through faith, trusting in Jesus as their Lord and Savior, will be able to stand in His presence when all is said and done.

But here is the irony: When Paul had a visitation from Jesus on the road to Damascus, he writes that he was taken up to paradise. He experienced an open vision of heaven and saw Jesus in all His glory. He saw things he could never speak about on this earth. The false teachers had been teaching the law of Moses instead of the gospel of Jesus Christ. There were more than six hundred rules and regulations in the Hebrew law, and some of the early Christians known as Judaizers were turning the gospel of grace into a gospel of works.

If we had to rely on our own goodness, no one could be saved. That is why God had to send His own Son to die on the cross for our sins. Whether it is six hundred laws, or ten commandments, or any other list of spiritual disciplines, none of these things will ever make you good enough for God. Yes, good works and godly living are important as evidence of the changes that have taken place in the believer's heart, but Paul says, "For by grace you have been saved through faith, and that not of yourselves; it is the gift of God" (Ephesians 2:8). The Christian life is not about what we can do for God, it is about what God, through his Son, has done for us. We must remember that God's mercy meets us first because (1) while we were yet in sin Christ died for us; (2) His grace created a love response in us for Him; (3) His grace teaches us not to sin; (4) His grace creates new desires in us; and (5) His grace energizes us with kingdom gifts and ministry.

## The Power of Humility

Isn't that an incredible message? We are saved by grace through faith—not by our good works but by simply believing in the Son of God, then living each day as beneficiaries of His redeeming grace. Through the eyes of faith we are able to see things that are not even in this world. They are spiritual truths that we learn to see through the eyes of faith. You and I have never seen Jesus; we have never seen Him in his physical body, but through the eyes of faith we see Him as our Lord and Savior. We know Him in an intimate and personal way, and we believe He has power to change things in our world. Through faith, we can change the atmosphere around us.

We know the blood of Christ was shed for us, and we know He rose from the dead. We know He is seated even now at the right hand of God the Father. How do we know all this? If you have accepted Jesus as Lord and Savior, you know it because He is living in your heart. He reveals Himself to you in your thoughts and prayers and fills you with the Holy Spirit. That is what it means to be saved by grace through faith.

You have probably noticed that in Paul's letters to the churches, he usually begins by laying out his credentials. He says in Romans, "Paul, a bondservant of Jesus Christ, called to be an apostle, separated to the gospel of God" (Romans 1:1). Even more impressive, in his letter to Titus he begins,

Paul, a bondservant of God and an apostle of Jesus Christ, according to the faith of God's elect and the acknowledgment of the truth which accords with godliness, in hope of eternal life which God, who cannot lie, promised before time began, but has in due time manifested His word through preaching, which was committed to me according to the commandment of God our Savior.

*verses 1–3*

That is quite a résumé, but Paul is not boasting. The emphasis is not on his own ability but on the office he was given by Jesus Himself. Before Paul ever mentions his authority as an apostle, he refers to himself as a bondservant and a slave. The emphasis is on the grace that has been entrusted into his hands, and not on what he can do with that gift. Paul was genuinely humble and often shy and embarrassed about his weaknesses, but he was bold for the kingdom of God. Unfortunately, a lot of Christians today seem to be looking for entertainment. Consequently, we have too many entertainers in the pulpits who are more than willing to bask in the limelight. But that was not Paul's way.

God grants grace and authority to those—both in the pulpits and the pews—who serve in humility, acknowledging that their authority comes from God alone. Paul doesn't say, "I can do all things because I'm a religious superstar!" He says, "I can do all things through Christ who strengthens me" (Philippians 4:13), and that is a word every believer ought to be able to speak. We can do all things because we are empowered by faith and obedience to the will of God.

There are times when we have to say, "God of grace, You know I am only human, but I am ready and willing to do whatever You call me to do. I express confidence in Your strength instead of my obvious natural limitations. I am trusting in You to make up the difference and give me the strength I need."

There are many days when I feel tired or weak or insecure about stepping out of my comfort zone, but I trust that God will give me the strength and courage I need, and that gives me boldness. Some folks may say they are too old, and others may say they are too young to stand up for what they believe. I remember one young man who told me he was going to dye his hair gray because he thought if he looked more mature, people would listen to him. But that was just an excuse. If the message is from God, then God can use anyone, young or old, rich or poor, big or small, to accomplish His will.

Some people try to use illness as an excuse. "I'm too sick," they say. They can name all sorts of health problems, but that is just an excuse. Illness needs to be dealt with, of course, but if God has called you to serve in some way, believe me, He can heal you. No matter what your issue may be. You just need to trust that He will supply the grace you need to accomplish His purpose through you when the time comes. That is a lesson I learned in some of my media appearances. If I had tried to perform in my own strength, there were times when I would have collapsed. But when I looked to Him for strength, God gave me the energy and the message He wanted me to speak.

*God grants grace and authority to those . . . who serve in humility.*

For some folks, time is the problem. They claim they do not have enough time, but there is always enough time to do the things you really care about. Others will say they do not have enough money to pursue God's call on their life, but that is another excuse. In Luke 11:23, God basically says, "No more excuses! Either you are with Me or you are against Me: so which will it be?"

Ultimately, the word of God will not be silenced. In Isaiah 55:11, God says, "So shall My word be that goes forth from My mouth; it shall not return to Me void, but it shall accomplish what I please, and it shall prosper in the thing for which I sent it." God wants to put you on the pathway to blessings, and all He asks is that you be willing and available. But if you refuse to stand up and be counted, He will find someone else to receive the blessings.

## The Hope of Transformation

Have you come to the point in your own walk of faith where God can trust you with His power? I am not talking about walking on water or raising the dead, but something a lot more practical. I am talking about the power of obedience, faithfulness and purity. I am talking about the power to control your emotions and behaviors, to live freely and openly as a child of God. Are you satisfied with the life you are living? Are you confident that God is happy with the choices you have been making? If not, you may need to change a few things.

Thanks to the threat of terrorism and other kinds of violence we see in our cities these days, there are surveillance cameras all over town, keeping track of what is going on and watching just about everything we do. Big Brother has his eyes on me and you. But let me ask you something: If you found out that somewhere in your hometown there were people watching how you live each day, in public and in private, would you be okay with that? Would you be satisfied with your Christian witness, or embarrassed?

The habits you have been living with are the result of decisions you made a long time ago. Over time those habits have transformed you into the person you are today. In that sense, you are a self-made man or woman. God is not really interested in how much money you make or how popular you are in your circle. Yes, God wants His children to enjoy peace and prosperity, but what He cares most about is your character. That is your foundation! Most folks want to skip the foundation and rush toward building a beautiful house. Jesus warned us about this in Luke 6:48–49. God is in the business of building character, and if we feel somebody poking at us and shoving us around a little bit, it just may be that God is trying to shape us into somebody with the kind of character He can actually use.

If that is where you are today, in a place where God is correcting and shaping you, you need to thank Him for His mercy. If God is poking at you, it is because He loves you and wants to transform you by the power of His grace. One of the most important lessons we can learn about the power of humility is that God does not want to hear our excuses. We all have our struggles. Whether we are young or old, sick or well, rich or poor, married or single or whatever else we are trying to blame for our problems, God does not need to hear about all that. He is calling us to something better.

We have seen what it was like for the apostle Paul. He overcame many limitations. There were seasons when he went hungry and barely had enough clothes to keep warm. He had some seasons with this world's treasures, when he had everything he needed. He had seen Jesus, and he was filled with wisdom and grace. Paul said, "I know both how to be abased, and I know how to abound" (Philippians 4:12 KJV). Some people think that his business, "Tentmakers for Jesus," may have had as many as 56 employees or ministry team members. The little the world could give Paul was meaningless, but the vision Jesus had given him was more than enough to transform his life.

> *God is trying to shape us into somebody with the kind of character He can actually use.*

Then, through the words Paul faithfully recorded in thirteen powerful letters included in the New Testament, untold millions around the world have discovered the secret of eternal life.

Now, I am not asking you to compare your own walk of faith to Paul's—none of us can live up to that standard. But these are some of the things I want to discuss with you in the following chapters, to help you focus on the calling God has placed on your life. So before we move on, I want you to consider these questions:

1. Have you had a life-changing experience or a defining moment in your life? If so, has it changed the way you live or given you a new sense of purpose? Has it changed your attitudes about yourself, your family or

your friends? And, most importantly, how has that experience affected your relationship with God?

2. What is the most important thing in your life today? Is it money, possessions, people, having a good time? Where does God fit in your top ten list? Is He at the top, the bottom or the middle of your list, or does He even make the list? If you are going to church on a regular basis, do the things you think about on Sunday affect the way you live the rest of the week? Are God's priorities reflected in your priorities? Would your family and friends agree that the values you say you admire are the ones you actually live by? Is your personal schedule a reflection of those priorities or does the inundation of what I call the "spam of living" distract you from being the person you really want to be? And, not to get too personal or anything, but what kind of person are you when no one is looking?

3. Finally, if you suddenly discovered a serious health issue or some other situation that presented you with a death sentence, what would you want to do before you die? Would you change anything about your life? Are there any situations to which you would want to bring closure through forgiveness or tying up loose ends before you leave this world? If you knew you had one day to live, what would you do? What would you say?

The fact is, we are all living under a death sentence of some kind, and one day every one of us will stand before Jesus Christ to give an account of our lives. What are you doing to prepare for that appointment? The good news is that you can transform your life and grace the atmosphere around you right now. You can find favor with God if you are willing to make the changes that will be required. Based on your answers to the previous questions, I hope you will have a strong sense of who you are as a child of God and what your life means to everyone around you. But I also hope you will take the time to pray through any area of concern that God may have opened up in your life.

It is vital to look at issues like these honestly and sincerely, with a willingness to make whatever changes are needed. If you want to make the most of this opportunity, choose one thing to do today that will demonstrate your desire to press forward with the work God is doing in your life. If you can do that with grace and humility, you may be surprised how much better you feel. A new day is about to dawn for you!

In the following chapters I will walk you through the rest of the process: to discover the true source of strength in your life, to reexamine the meaning of grace and to see where true and lasting love comes from. Then I will discuss what real success in life is all about. Following that, I will share what you can do, with God's help, when everything seems to be falling apart, whether it is a lost job, a broken friendship or some other challenge in your life.

Finally, I will speak briefly about what is going on in the secret places of your heart. Sooner or later everyone comes to the point where they need a fresh start. It is tempting to believe that our problems lie somewhere else, or with someone else. The fact is, most of our problems have their roots right where we live, in our own hearts and minds and in our own behavior. External problems can play havoc with our plans, but if we are really honest about it, we usually find answers by taking a look at what is going on in our own hearts.

If you have come to the point where you are ready to hear what God has to say, I would like to share some good news. Know that whoever you are and wherever you may be in your life at this moment, God has answers for your situation. They are available now. And in the following chapters we will continue our look at six steps to transforming your world. All I ask you to do now is to turn the page and think seriously about what it could mean to make a fresh start with God in the driver's seat. Then come along with me for a short and potentially life-changing journey to your spiritual breakthrough.

# WITH WINGS LIKE EAGLES

*Step Two: Trust God and Be Someone
He Can Trust*

*N*obody wants to be a weakling. It is only natural to want to be seen as strong and capable. As a young man, I was a wrestler and football player. At one time I even had a professional football contract with the New England Patriots in the NFL. I was strong and athletic, and the last thing I wanted was for anybody to think of me as weak. But when I look back at my life, some of my most fulfilling experiences have come not through skill or strength but through weakness.

Let me give you an example. During some of the roughest days of my chemotherapy treatments, I was invited to the studios of CNN in Washington, D.C., for a live TV interview. This has happened several times over the years. I was honored to be asked on this occasion, and there were important things I wanted to discuss, but when I arrived for the interview I was utterly exhausted and unable to speak.

Then, as we were parking outside the studios, I started coughing uncontrollably. I remember getting out of the van and praying, "Lord, I stand in my weakness. May You stand in Your strength." What I meant was, "Lord, I'm getting ready to drag myself inside that place for an important interview, and if You don't show up and pull me through it, this could be the mother of all big-time screw-ups." I couldn't put two thoughts together, let alone two coherent sentences.

Fortunately, God did show up and pulled me through. He heard my prayer, and just as I was walking onto the set, my physical symptoms subsided. God gave me the strength I needed at that moment and I was able to say exactly what I needed to say. It came off very well, but the honor belonged not to me but to God. What I was living out was the principle that Paul was declaring when he said, "I will not boast, except in my infirmities" (2 Corinthians 12:5).

God cannot trust a person with a proud and haughty spirit to do His will, which is why the Bible warns us repeatedly against the sin of pride. The psalmist tells us that God reserves His blessings for the man or woman with a willing spirit and a contrite heart (see Psalm 51:17). In the walk of faith we often gain strength through weakness. As we have already seen, the apostle Paul's weakness was the key to his usefulness to God: "I take pleasure in infirmities, in reproaches, in needs, in persecutions, in distresses, for Christ's sake. For when I am weak, then I am strong" (2 Corinthians 12:10).

We can be around people we see as strong and self-reliant, when in fact the strength we see is not really their own strength but the power of God working through them.

As a varsity wrestler in high school, I was fortunate to be named to the first-team, all-city squad. I won a lot of matches, but it took important lessons to get to that level. Early on, I struggled with some of the moves. I started out trying to push the big guys around using my strength. It wasn't for lack of trying, because no one on the team worked harder than I did. But all my effort was to no avail until my coach pulled me aside one day. He said if I could focus my energy on two basic moves—the arm drag/duck under and a pivoting stand-up—I would do fine. Both moves were based on my speed. And both moves made me look and feel vulnerable. But you know what? Coach was right. By concentrating on two moves that had been some of the hardest for me to master, I became a pretty good wrestler. By changing my focus I changed my outcome.

> *God cannot trust a person with a proud and haughty spirit to do His will.*

This is an important principle in the Christian life as well. Our goal is to "win" for God. By becoming vulnerable and depending on God, we are able to discover the places where God can do His work through us. Fortunately, we have several examples of how the process works—the Bible is full of them. The patriarch Jacob, who was the son of Isaac and grandson of Abraham, struggled with a serious character flaw, and he found himself in a jam more than once because of his tendency to take advantage of people. But despite this weakness, God saw Jacob as someone He could use, and over time He transformed Jacob's life.

The story of Jacob's journey, found in the book of Genesis, is fascinating. At one point Jacob was so brash that he dared to wrestle with the angel of God, demanding that the angel give him a blessing. They wrestled all night, and somehow Jacob managed to wear the angel down and keep him engaged. Jacob did not win the struggle; it says he "prevailed" (32:25) and made his heart known to the Lord. The Lord decided to grant Jacob's request, but as a result he walked with a limp the rest of his life. Jacob wanted to know that God would guarantee or promise to bless him, and that's why he refused to let the angel go until he received the blessing. But, at the same time, God was checking Jacob out. And when God saw that He could trust Jacob—saw his passion, his focus, his heart—He gave him a new name and made him one of the patriarchs of Israel. After that, God was able to use Jacob in a mighty way.

Jacob's story shows desperation, not audacity. His fear of the consequences of being a trickster is what the Lord made him face. In my life-and-death struggle with cancer, I, too, had to examine my motives. Jacob had depended too much on his obvious, natural giftings of brainpower and cunning. God commended his willpower and tenacity, but He left Jacob with a limp as a lesson—to Jacob and to us: God's power should not be an afterthought but the first thought. Compared with God's power, our natural ability is never enough to get "God results." Our limitations, like a limp, remind us that if we are going to win our next wrestling match, God will have to do the heavy lifting—the hard stuff.

So let me ask: Have you reached the point in your own walk of faith where you can trust God with your life? Can you trust Him with your health, the safety of your family, your career? If you are praying for a breakthrough, you will need to work on your relationship with God. He is faithful and just, but He is not a genie in a bottle or some kind of wishing well. He is not even your sweet old grandpa looking out for you. He is the sovereign Lord, and He loves you

> *God is not a genie in a bottle or some kind of wishing well.*

with an everlasting love and wants you to experience blessings in your life. But again, the trust relationship has to work both ways. God has to know He can trust you to walk humbly before Him in the way that you should go (see Isaiah 48:17).

Jesus lived a perfect, sinless life. He is the standard we all ought to be aiming for, but remember that it was His death on the cross, carried out in His human weakness, that transformed the Son of God into the Redeemer of mankind. The Christian's goal is to be conformed to the image of Christ (see Romans 8:29). We do not need to die for anybody, of course. Christ died for our sins once and for all. And yes, some of the changes we are asked to make in order to become more like Jesus may feel like death. But it is essential to start with a willing spirit and trust in God.

## New Life in Christ

All this is what the apostle calls putting off the old man and putting on the new man. Paul writes, "Do not be conformed to this world, but be transformed by the renewing of your mind, that you may prove what is that good and acceptable and perfect will of God" (Romans 12:2).

One worldly barrier to a new life in Christ is an "I've-got-it-made" attitude. We get a couple of mortgage payments in the bank, a diploma on the wall, a pretty good job, the house of our dreams, and we get the idea we do not need anybody's help. We get a false perception of strength.

You and I may be the envy of the neighborhood, but we are still weaklings compared to the problems the world can throw at us. No matter how well off we may be, we are at the mercy of the next recession or natural disaster or family emergency that comes along. In our own strength, we are powerless. The only security in this world is a posture of dependence, relying upon divine grace and placing our trust in the infinite power and love of an all-powerful and all-loving God.

Over the years we have seen a number of gospel recording artists who had a dynamic anointing on their lives and ministries, but somewhere along the way something changed. It has happened to some well-known preachers, too. They are still famous, still making money, still drawing a crowd. Some of them are still appearing on television or doing concerts, but tragically they have drifted away. They have compromised their beliefs and fallen for the pleasures of this world.

Consequently, they have lost the anointing and sense of power in their message and ministry. Unfortunately, what we call "anointing" is often human gifting and talent.

Nonetheless, many of us *are* longing for the genuine presence of the Holy Spirit in our lives. And yes, despite the cynics, true anointing is still available. When we are trusting God and serving Him faithfully each day, the Holy Spirit blesses our lives and fills us with hope, a sense of purpose and a continuous flow of spiritual refreshment. But if we become distracted, if we allow fame and fortune to become our god or if we begin to think that we can do it all on our own without God's help, we can lose the ability to distinguish between the applause of the world and the authentic blessings of God.

> *Despite the cynics, true anointing is still available.*

How many times have you seen friends slipping away from the truth of God's Word for a little dip in the pool of lust? *Oh, don't worry,* they think. *It's just this once!* Or some will say, "Surely God wants me to be happy, doesn't He!" The answer is, "Yes, He does, but your idea of happiness is all messed up."

The best and most lasting happiness in this life comes from obedience to the will of God. As the old hymn says, "Trust and obey, for there's no other way to be happy in Jesus, but to trust and obey." You may think you have all the answers and you don't need anybody's help. But sooner or later you are going to need supernatural strength to get out of a bad situation, no matter how hard you try. And when that happens there is only one place to turn. This was the lesson King David had to learn. The Holy Spirit will guide our footsteps if we are willing to turn our lives around and follow Him. This is certainly true for new believers, but it is also true for those in the household of faith who have grown stiff and inflexible and perhaps a little forgetful over the years.

You probably know some folks who have been believers so long they have forgotten how dependent they were on Christ when they first got saved. Their faith was strong then. It was new and fresh, and every day was a wonderful adventure. But over time they settled into a routine, and instead of following Jesus with hope and anticipation, they just kept following the rules. Sometimes we have faith in our faith techniques, don't we? We make all the right moves according to the last sermon we heard or the last book we read instead of relying on Christ to guide our footsteps each day. We become legalistic and inflexible, depending on our religiosity rather than the true and living God.

The walk of faith ought to be filled with joy. If we are truly living as Jesus called us to live, we ought to be excited about following Him in good times and bad. I believe we have come to the place where God wants to change the atmosphere around us. He wants to transform the world we live in. But if you and I want to be part of what God is doing in the world, we have to be open to how He moves.

We have to put on "the new man," as Paul says, in order to be "renewed in knowledge" and transformed into the image of Christ (Colossians 3:10). When we do that, the old selfish and self-centered ways start to fade away and we truly become "new creatures in Christ." There are times when following the rules is the best response, but the walk of faith ought to be a vital and stimulating daily adventure.

## Learning to Trust

God assures us His grace is sufficient for our needs, whatever our needs may be (see 2 Corinthians 12:9). In fact, for men and women who are full of faith, the Lord fills up their dry places with the fullness of His power. He does not have to give us anything else. He does not have to remove the thorn in our flesh because we already have the ability to deal with that issue. You have the ability to get out of the mess you are in. You have the ability to transform your home, your job, your family and your way of life. But it goes much further than that. As believers, we have the ability to take back our city. We have the ability to take back our community. We have the ability to take back our finances. We have the ability to turn a situation around, regardless of what the situation may be, because we know that God's strength is made perfect through our weakness.

But what does it mean to be made perfect? The word *perfect* here means "full" or "complete." In other words, the full manifestation of His power becomes available when we recognize what little children express when they sing, "Little ones to Him belong; they are weak, but He is strong."

But let me illustrate the principle this way. Imagine that I am trying to get water out of an old pump well. I have the strength to move the handle up and down, but no water is coming out. God is saying, "You don't have any water because you are not weak enough. And if you keep on pumping that handle you're never going to get any water. As long as you think you can handle this problem all by yourself, I am just going to let you go. But when you realize that you need Me to step in, then I will open the valve and let the water flow."

The problem is that we keep trying to deal with the issues in our lives in our own strength. We do not want to admit we need God's help. We think we can handle it, so we do not let God move the obstacles out of the way. He has told us what it takes to overcome our problems. He says, "My grace is sufficient for you. . . ." (2 Corinthians 12:9). But we will never be able to open the valve and release the flow of blessing until we call upon Him to reveal His grace.

God will never share His glory with anyone, and He doesn't need our help to accomplish His will. But because He loves us with an everlasting love, He graciously allows us to participate in His plans on this earth. He has made us agents of His grace and compassion in a fallen world. Paul writes in Galatians that the good works we do, sharing the love of God with others, are the evidence of Christ Jesus living and working in us. He says, "I have been crucified with Christ; it is no longer I who live, but Christ lives in me; and the life which I now live in the flesh I live by faith in the Son of God, who loved me and gave Himself for me" (2:20).

*The problem is . . . we do not want to admit we need God's help.*

We can frustrate the grace of God, Paul says, when we try to do things by some other standard. There were teachers in Paul's day who insisted that Christians had to follow the Hebrew laws, but Paul points out that any attempt to earn our salvation by strict legalism or good works of any kind would make the cross of Christ pointless: "I do not set aside the grace of God; for if righteousness comes through the law, then Christ died in vain" (Galatians 2:21).

The point is, we cannot add anything to what Jesus has already done and we must allow what He has done to have full sway in our lives. This is what Paul means when he says, "For by grace you have been saved through faith, and that not of yourselves; it is the gift of God, not of works, lest anyone should boast" (Ephesians 2:8–9). We are saved by the grace of God through our faith in Jesus Christ.

Let me give you another illustration. You have undoubtedly come across over-the-counter medicines that claim to be "time-released," meaning you take the pill now and it automatically releases the prescribed dosage as you need it. Paul wants us to know that God has already released the power of the gospel into our lives, but when we try to earn our salvation by our own efforts, we interfere with God's time-release formula of grace.

Say you are in a middle of a problem and you ask God for help. God says He has already sent you the help you need, but you are running all over the place trying to solve your problem your way, and it is not working. When you take some other "medicine," you are just canceling out the medicine of grace that is already in your life. This is why Paul says he glories in weakness, because it allows God's power to grow strong. Until we intentionally admit our weakness and celebrate His strength, God's power cannot come forth. And until we recognize that we are not in control, He will simply say, "Okay, go ahead and do it your way and see how that works out."

God is asking us whether or not we will we allow Him to accomplish His plan for our lives. Many times Christians find themselves in trouble and they start praying for a miracle. But Paul is saying we do not need the miracles we think we need. We need to learn how to work with what God has already given us. Like the water well I mentioned earlier, we need to take our hands off the pump so the grace of God can flow into our lives.

This is what I have called "gracing your atmosphere." In other words, your world can be transformed by what God has already put into your world. He may then direct you to march around "Jericho" seven times and shout. It is all about using what has been given to you, the way God ordained for it to be used. Too many Christians are living beneath the level of privilege that God has planned for them. Why in the world did Paul go through all of those hardships? One reason was that God wanted to use Paul's example to teach us how we are to respond in times of crisis. Paul says his thorn in the flesh was a messenger of Satan sent to keep him from being vain or conceited (see 2 Corinthians 12:7). So instead of boasting about his great learning or his authority as an apostle, he learned to trust in the grace of God and yield to the direction of God.

Have you ever wondered why, in some of the most powerful stories in the Bible, God does things in the most impossible way? Take the story of Gideon in the book of Judges, for example. God finds a strong young man who is honorable and trustworthy. The angel of the Lord appears to Gideon and calls him "a mighty man of valor." But when the angel tells Gideon He has an important job for him, he responds in much the same way Moses did at the burning bush, saying, in essence, "Lord, surely You can't be talking to me! You have the wrong guy!" But the angel reassures Gideon he has been chosen by God to be the general of His army, to go up against the Midianites.

The dialogue does not end there. Gideon and the Lord work through a couple of confirmation exercises—Gideon wants to be sure it is the Lord really speaking to him. But when Gideon overhears a Midianite's dream, his enemy's conviction about his destiny becomes a prophetic word from God. It is true that sometimes the enemy's attack on us is so vicious, he seems to have more confidence in our potential than we do. At the end of this process of renewing Gideon's mind—through a prophetic word from a couple of soldiers in the enemy's camp—he is finally willing to step out in faith and calls for his friends. Thirty thousand men show up. And just when Gideon start thinking victory is possible, God interrupts his euphoria and tells him he has too many soldiers. God wants to be sure that, when the Israelites win, nobody can say it is because Gideon had raised an army of thirty thousand men. He wants people to know it was God's power and strength that gave Israel the victory. So He orders Gideon to cut the army down to three hundred.

Can you imagine how Gideon must have felt? Compared to the enemy they were facing, the Israelite army of three hundred soldiers was a joke. The text says the Midianite army was "lying in the valley as numerous as locusts; and their camels were without number, as the sand by the seashore in multitude" (Judges 7:12). Gideon probably thought God was setting him up for disaster. The whole thing was impossible by human standards. Gideon knew he could never defeat the Midianites and the Amelikites with three hundred men. He would be dead by sundown. Only God could save him now, but that was precisely the point.

Anticipating Gideon's reaction, God assures him once again that they would win, but only when the Israelite army was weak enough for God to receive the glory. Once Gideon whittled his army down to size, God could open up the full throttle of His power. It was a situation in which Gideon had no choice but to be humble and place his trust in God. He would have to trust God to do the impossible, and when he followed the instructions of the angel of the Lord, the Israelites were able to surprise the Midianite army and win the most astonishing victory—not through their own strength or cunning but through their weakness and their trust in the Lord.

## The Gift of Grace

Frankly, there are some folks who know too much Bible to experience a miracle like that. They have been doing things their own way far too long to let God supernaturally change their plans. Preachers might be the worst. We have been to seminary to understand how God works and how He moves. There are times when the Lord may supernaturally appear and require something from us or lead us in a certain way, but too often, like Gideon, we find ourselves explaining to God why He supposedly cannot do what He wants to do. This is because we get a little confused. We think we are supposed to be the strong ones. But God says it is only in a place of weakness where we have to let go of the controls and rely upon His grace that God's purposes can be accomplished.

> *Friends were telling me to defeat the illness . . . by all the traditional means, without turning the whole thing over to God.*

I learned some hard lessons in this regard early in my battle with cancer. I had been preaching around the country about what happens during an extreme spiritual makeover. I shared how God can appear to us through trials and changes we experience in life. But, at the same time, some friends were telling me to defeat the illness that had invaded my body by all the traditional means, without turning the whole thing over to God.

For a time they were sure I could defeat the cancer with drugs; then they told me that chemo would do it; and after that they said surgery and all kinds of radical nutritional treatments would cure me. But it wasn't until, in the silence of my hospital room, surrounded by my family, that the God factor really kicked in. That is when the healing began.

I think it is interesting that the Chinese word for *crisis* is made up of two different characters, the first meaning "danger" and the other related to the idea of "opportunity." That is a great way of looking at it. Whenever we face a crisis—financial, physical, spiritual or something else—the danger almost always comes with some sort of opportunity. The opportunity may not be obvious, but during those times God wants to release His power into our lives, and He may be using that period of adversity to shape and mold us into the men and women He wants us to become.

We see this in Hosea 2:15, where God says He will open a door of hope in the Valley of Achor. The word *Achor* means trouble, and very often the place of trouble actually opens a door of hope and opportunity. You will not open the door; God opens it. God will also open a door of expectation, so that His grace can flow over your life. If you read the passage in Hosea in its entirety, it says we will sing once again, as in the days of our youth. God will turn our sorrow into singing, restoring hope and expectation, pouring His blessings into our lives.

Before I get into the four distinctive dimensions of grace that the Lord walked me through in my spiritual makeover, I must explain how I understand grace as a force in Christian life. For centuries believers have been debating how God's grace works and how to access it.

Today there are essentially two foundational schools of thought concerning grace. The first is the Calvinist belief developed by John Calvin (1509–1564), who was born in Noyon, France. His theology centers on the concept of the supreme sovereignty of God. The acrostic TULIP is often used to remember the elements of the belief:

Total depravity of man,
Unconditional election,
Limited atonement,
Irresistible grace, and the
Perseverance of the saints.

The second view is called Arminianism; it is very different from Calvinism and is based on the biblical teachings of Jacobus Arminius (1560–1609), who studied under John Calvin's son-in-law. He later went into pastoral ministry in Amsterdam and then was a professor teaching the book of Romans.

Arminius began to focus on conditional election based on God's foreknowledge of man's free will to cooperate with God, resistible grace, Christ's universal atonement, and that salvation could potentially be lost. In other words, Arminians believe that you and I can "frustrate the grace of God" (Galatians 2:2) or miss out on His plan thorough disobedience or rebellion.

I lean toward the Arminian school of thought with one big exception: If someone really is born again, it is probably very difficult to pry ourselves out of the hands of God. But salvation is not supposed to be a destination; it is supposed to be a starting point. Nonetheless, this means a lot of Christian people are—through deception, ignorance or disobedience—only achieving 60 percent, 30 percent or less of the joy, satisfaction or rewards of bearing God's fruit and doing His will (see Matthew 13:8 or Mark 4:20).

To understand how the grace of God often appears to us, I would like to take a closer look in the next couple of pages at four types of grace that come forth from God when we are confronted by challenges and changes in our lives.

The first kind is what I call *survival grace*. The theological name for this dimension of grace is divine providence, and it is taught in some shape or form in every major religion and all Christian denominations. Through divine providence the

Lord shuts the door to Satan's plans to snuff us out or to wipe out our families. Revivalist John Wesley in a message based on Luke 12:7 proclaimed the virtues of survival grace: "And as this all-wise, all-gracious Being created all things, so he sustains all things. He is the Preserver as well as the Creator of everything that exists. . . . Now it must be that he knows everything he has made, and everything he preserves, from moment to moment; otherwise, he could not preserve it; he could not continue to it the going which he has given it. . . ."

Survival grace often comes in dramatic or emergency situations, when you don't have time to cry out to Jesus for help. It may be when a car swerves dangerously into your path but by the grace of God you manage to dodge it. Or it may be apparent in a long-standing financial problem. With no strategy to get out of the mess, you fear personal ruin, but then you discover you are able to make that monthly payment and hold on to your house. By any rational analysis, you should have been wiped out, but God intervened.

This dimension of grace is not automatic. You cannot set your watch by it, but if you are walking with God daily and doing your best to be the man or woman He can use, God may surprise you with a gift of survival grace. When God upholds you by His mighty hand, there can be no doubt where that power came from. Just as He upheld the children of Israel in the wilderness, He can lift you out of the miry pit. Moses led the Israelites through the wilderness for forty years, and they were rude and rebellious the whole time. But because of His faithfulness and His grace, God fed them, clothed them and protected them from the wild beasts.

That same survival grace is available to us today. Survival grace is implemented by God in what the Scripture calls a *Kairos* moment—a strategic time when God wants to change the order of things for His own purposes. For a moment, He stops heaven and earth. He stops the decline. He changes the nature of the problem and allows there to be some form of redemption. No wonder we call Him Savior.

We need the second dimension of grace, which I call *visionary grace* or being filled with the Holy Spirit, in order to walk in intimacy and cooperate with the power of the Holy Spirit. From a theological point of view, this is an extreme oversimplification of our need to walk in personal intimacy with the Lord through the Holy Spirit and for the Lord to open our eyes to see new dimensions of our personal callings. Theologian Charles Ryrie has written, "From the viewpoint of practice and experience, the filling with the Spirit is the most important aspect of the doctrine of the Holy Spirit." The following Scriptures suggest that the power of the early church was based upon the power of the Holy Spirit: Ephesians 5:18; Acts 2:4, 33; Acts 4:8, 31; 6:3; 13:9.

*Survival grace often comes in dramatic or emergency situations.*

What it means to be filled with the Holy Spirit can differ doctrinally from one Christian denomination to another. Unfortunately, many of our denominations treat this area as though there is a checklist of forbidden experiences. I do not intend to explore controversial topics here. Every believer's experience of being filled with the Spirit is experiential and, to a large extent, subjective. The Holy Spirit will endow each believer who yields to His influence gifts, fruit, anointing, indwelling and power, to name just a few dynamics.

For me, in the months during my cancer treaments, having my short-term memory nearly erased and losing nearly seventy pounds, I became much more intimate with the Lord through the Scriptures, praise and prayer. I was filled with the Spirit in a fresh way. I also found that the Lord gave me a dramatically new sense of purpose and spiritual passion. All of this mirrored Philippians 2:13: "For it is God who works in you to will and to act according to his good purpose" (NIV1984).

Visionary grace comes when God shows you what to do in a critical situation. I will deal with this subject in greater depth in the next chapter, but for now it is important to remember that God knows our hearts better than we know ourselves, and He knows our needs before we do. As with survival grace, visionary grace is not available on demand, but there are times when God will intervene in our situation and allow us to see in advance what needs to be done.

A third dimension of grace, *transitional grace*, is released as we enter into a personal covenant with the Lord around our unique calling. In the Word of God, at least nine covenants are presented (in addition to marriage). In marriage, as Christians, we invite the Lord to be an invisible partner in this union. The nine covenants are as follows:

- the Edenic Covenant (see Genesis 1–2)
- the Adamic Covenant (see Genesis 3)
- the Noahic Covenant (see Genesis 6–9)

- the Abrahamic Covenant (see Genesis 12–22)
- the Mosaic Covenant (see Exodus 19-40; Galatians 3:24)
- the Palestinian Covenant (see Deuteronomy 27–33)
- the Davidic Covenant (see 2 Samuel 7; Psalm 89; Psalm 132)
- the New Covenant (see Jeremiah 31:31–34; Hebrews 8)
- the Everlasting Covenant (see 1 Chronicles 16:7; Isaiah 55:3; Genesis 17:7)

As the Lord leads us out of our crisis, He brings us into the grace of making a personal covenant with Him. God uses covenants to specify terms and conditions under which He will move and work within someone's life. When the Israelites moved into the Promised Land, they had the fighting age men circumcised as a sign of renewing their national covenant with God. He promised to use His power to plant them in the land of promise. These personal covenants are needed when the Lord is taking us to a new level. We are all part of the new covenant.

A good demonstration of this transitional grace can be seen in the lives of the Israelites, when their daily supply of manna stopped just as they were entering the Promised Land. God had provided food and guidance for them for forty years. You might say He was their heavenly GPS system, leading them with a pillar of cloud in the daytime and a pillar of fire by night. But when they entered the Promised Land they needed to undergo some major changes, including learning how to cultivate crops and raise animals. Consequently, God guided them by His grace through a time of transition.

Our nation and world is in the midst of a complex and challenging transition at this moment. The economy is being shaken. Our culture often seems to be imploding. There is terror and violence on a level never seen before, and many of our families are in turmoil. In such a time we need to understand that transitional grace comes to us when we place our trust in the One who can restore order to our confused and corrupt world.

God has answers. Our fathers and mothers knew this, and as long as the nation remembered to give Him the honor and glory He deserves, we were "a shining city on a hill." But when we began removing any mention of God from our public life, stripping every reference to God and the Bible from our schools, and acting as if the faith of our fathers no longer has any meaning, we began a slow and painful descent into chaos. If we are to have any hope of restoring the fabric of this nation and regaining our confidence and security, we will need to remember how we got to this place and regain our trust in Him.

> *Personal covenants are needed when the Lord is taking us to a new level.*

Our coins say "In God we trust," which ought to be the personal motto of every American. It is only because of the wisdom and grace of God that so great a nation came into being in the first place, and we will need His sovereign guidance if we are to survive. Without a change in the way our leaders approach problems, there may be no way out of our dilemma. This is why I hope you will be praying, not only for your own personal transformation but for a large dose of God's transitional grace for this country in the months and years ahead.

## Establishment Grace

The last dimension of grace I want to mention here is *establishment grace*, which is somewhat broader in application than the other three. Establishment grace is essentially the idea of walking with God in personal holiness, or what theologians would call "sanctification."

In the Old Testament, sanctification primarily meant to be set apart. The idea would be that believers were set apart unto God's purposes and away from the world's agenda. Most scholars believe that the New Testament word for sanctification strongly describes a relationship with God that helps Christians live the moral and ethical dimension that pleases God. The best book I have come across on this topic is *Five Views on Sanctification.*[1] Five diverse theological views of sanctification are examined in depth. Each one of the advocates for their perspective believes that holiness in thought, word and deed is God's goal for His people.

The term *personal holiness* sounds so harsh and judgmental to many folks in our generation that popular teachers rarely broach the topic. Modern-day "Bereans" hardly ever pick this topic to study. It is a shame that the pursuit of holiness is being so neglected. As a result, the inner joy, peace and power of God that has historically accompanied giants

1. Melvin E. Dieter, Anthony A. Hoekema, Stanley M. Horton, J. Robertson McQuilkin, John F. Walvoord, *Five Views on Sanctification*, ed. Stanley N. Gundry (Grand Rapids: Zondervan, 1987).

in the faith is missing in our generation. After Pentecost, even the apostle Peter walked in such a realm of personal obedience to the Word of God and the promptings of the Holy Spirit that both the gifts and the fruit of the Holy Spirit abounded in him. Let's briefly review just two of these schools of thought—just as we did the doctrine of grace earlier in this book.

## 1. The Arminian/Wesleyan View of Sanctification

For John Wesley, the ultimate goal of sanctification was "to renew men's and women's hearts in [God's] image."[2] Wesley believed that faith works by love, as Galatians 5:6 says, and that the grace of God brings the practical fruit of holiness into our lives. Wesley also believed that love was the true measure of sanctification. In other words, the more you loved God, the more you would want to live for Him.

Sanctification is fueled by love and sustained by intimacy and love—"faith working through love" (Galatians 5:6) was not faith to get things, but rather faith to become more like Jesus. Wesley and his followers taught that sanctification is received by faith just as salvation is. When a Christian cries out to the Lord for the power to live right, according to the old-time Methodist mind the Holy Spirit takes away their "bondage to sin" or iniquitous character roots and replaces them with a "bent to loving obedience."[3]

2. Melvin E. Dieter, "The Wesleyan Perspective," in *Five Views on Sanctification*, 15.
3. John Wesley, quoted in ibid., 25.

Wesley often said that Christians should not be "content with any religion which does not imply the destruction of all the works of the devil, that is of all sin."[4] We can fulfill God's law of love in this life, despite all the failings and imperfections of the world. This is what he called the "optimism of grace."

## 2. The Reformed/Calvinist View of Sanctification

John Calvin, whose teaching we touched on briefly earlier in this work, is considered the greatest theologian of the Reformed tradition. Reformed teachers believed the goal of sanctification was the believer's personal perfection or maturity and to give our lives "to the praise of His glory" (Ephesians 1:12).

Reformed teachers say there are three essential requirements for sanctification:

1. A growing personal union with Christ. We are sanctified by the truth. The Bible is "one of the chief means whereby God sanctifies His people."[5]

2. Faith. Faith helps us to live in union with Christ.

3. Acknowledgment that we are no longer mastered by sin. This reality results in the production of fruit in the life of the Christian.

"Definitive sanctification" of the Calvinists differs from Wesley's entire sanctification in two important ways. First,

4. Ibid., 13.
5. Anthony A. Hoekema, "The Reformed Perspective," in *Five Views on Sanctitifcation*, 64.

unlike Wesley, the Calvinists do not believe that sanctification can produce a state of sinless perfection in the Christian. Reformed teachers assert that Christians will always "struggle against sin, and they will sometimes fall into sin."[6] In other words, a true believer is genuinely a new creature but he or she is not fully transformed into Christ's image. Second, definitive sanctification does not occur in an experience subsequent to salvation but rather coincides with it.

At the turn of the twentieth century, when the Pentecostal/charismatic movement started, the defining aspect was its emphasis on manifestations such as speaking in tongues and prophecy. As it pertains to sanctification and holiness, these Pentecostals disagreed over how sanctification occurred in the life of a believer. Holiness Pentecostals asserted that before one can receive the baptism of the Holy Spirit,[7] they had to first undergo the experience of entire sanctification.

Other Pentecostals (like those who later formed the Assemblies of God and Foursquare denominations) believed that faith in Christ was the only precondition for receiving the baptism of the Holy Spirit. These groups emphasized spiritual gift manifestations (such as speaking in tongues and prophecy) as the initial sign of the infilling of the Holy Spirit. After these gateway events, believers were expected to allow the Holy Spirit to bring a measure of progressive holiness (see 2 Corinthians 3:18).

John the Baptist's declaration in Matthew 3:11–12 is also foundational to their theology:

6. Ibid., 74.
7. A permanent empowering of the Holy Spirit often evidenced by speaking in tongues that Christians typically receive sometime after conversion.

I indeed baptize you with water unto repentance, but He who is coming after me is mightier than I, whose sandals I am not worthy to carry. He will baptize you with the Holy Spirit and fire. His winnowing fan is in His hand, and He will thoroughly clean out His threshing floor, and gather His wheat into the barn; but He will burn up the chaff with unquenchable fire.

In Joshua 7, we read about Joshua's army being defeated in a place called Ai. They lost the battle because they did not follow God's earlier instructions regarding nearby Jericho.

You may recall that Jericho was the first city God gave the Israelites when they came to the Promised Land. The old spiritual says, "Joshua fit the battle of Jericho, and the walls came tumblin' down." Jericho was special to the Jewish people and to God, and Joshua was instructed to give everything from that place back to God as a tithe. In return, God promised to give them victory after victory, and everybody did what they were supposed to do. Everybody but one man, that is. Achan took silver and gold and some Babylonian garments for himself. And, of course, the result was a disaster.

As part of our covenant with God, the tithe is supposed to be devoted to God. You may remember the exhortation of Malachi:

> "Bring all the tithes into the storehouse, that there may be food in My house, and try Me now in this," says the LORD of hosts, "if I will not open for you the windows of heaven and pour out for you such blessing that there will not be room enough to receive it."
>
> *Malachi 3:10*

This is a key aspect of establishment grace. The principle of the tithe, as ancient as the Bible itself, was established by God for His glory and our good.

Unfortunately, like the Israelites at Jericho, many Christians believe they can take the things that are devoted to God and use them for themselves. And we wonder why we find ourselves in a mess so often. In the Old Testament, if someone ate the tithe instead of giving it to the Lord, they were allowed to restore the tithe with a 20-percent penalty. Funny, that sounds a lot like our credit card debt today, doesn't it? It is as if God is saying, "The tithe belongs to Me. Either give it to Me freely or I will take it from you another way."

As I said, the principle of giving a tithe to God is an instrumental part of our covenant with God. If we do not handle that covenant correctly, He cannot bless the rest of our finances. The treasures of Jericho were supposed to be the Israelites' tithe to God. Unfortunately, the defeat at Ai taught them a very hard lesson. Later, as the Israelites moved forward, God gave them other absolutes, and the benefits they gained from following those principles were examples of God's establishment grace.

What I have been trying to illustrate in this chapter is that we serve an infinitely good and gracious God. He loves us so much He sent His Son to die for our sins. He longs for us to thrive and enjoy the riches of His grace, and He has promised blessings when we come to Him with humility and trust. Nowhere is the promise of blessing stated more clearly than in the prophecy of Isaiah, which says:

Have you not known? Have you not heard? The everlasting God, the LORD, the Creator of the ends of the earth, neither faints nor is weary. His understanding is unsearchable. He gives power to the weak, and to those who have no might He increases strength. Even the youths shall faint and be weary, and the young men shall utterly fall, but those who wait on the LORD shall renew their strength; they shall mount up with wings like eagles, they shall run and not be weary, they shall walk and not faint.

*Isaiah 40:28–31 NKJV*

This is such an encouraging promise, how could anyone fail to be convinced? God is saying that by placing your trust in His mercy and grace you will be able to soar above adversity, temptations and disappointments of every kind, with wings like eagles. What a remarkable image.

We have been given a prescription for a time-release formula that can bring success into our lives. If we want to experience genuine growth and transformation, we need to claim God's promises by living for Him and drawing closer to Him every day of our lives. Rest assured, you can have complete confidence in the grace and goodness of God. You can trust Him with your life. But to experience the joy that Christ has to offer, He needs to know He can trust you, too.

# ═ 3 ═

# LOVE BEYOND MEASURE

## Step Three: Be an Emissary of God's Love

*T*t is such a simple word. *Love.* We hear it all the time and in every conceivable way. Unfortunately, Hollywood has made a mockery of it. It is all over the television and the grocery-store tabloids. The secular world has perverted the word and made it into something erotic and unclean. Even popular music has lost the mystery of deep, romantic love.

The Christian writer C. S. Lewis thought the subject of love was so important he wrote a series of essays and several books on the subject, trying to explain what love is and why it is so essential to the walk of faith. The apostle John writes, "God is love, and he who abides in love abides in God, and God in him" (1 John 4:16). Do you hear what the apostle is saying? *God is love.* To experience true love you need God in your life. And if you want to experience the favor of God, you must abide in

79

His love. But how do you do that when the concept of love has been so badly misused?

If you want to please someone you love, you do things they appreciate. You will be thoughtful, courteous, generous and kind. You pay attention to them when they speak to you, and you show them the respect they deserve. But if you do that for your loved ones now, what sort of service do you owe the God who made you—the God who, the Bible says, is love?

Learning to receive and then to imitate the love of God is not merely another aspect of the journey of faith. It is one of the most important steps to finding your true calling and fulfilling your destiny. Walking and living in love is so important that Jesus said it will be the hallmark and defining sign that you and I are truly His. To make this point another way, the apostle John said that hatred or the absence of love was the major sign that we did not know God at all (see 1 John 4:20). Despite this declaration, racism, denominational prejudice and many other divisions exist within the Body of Christ.

Jesus boldly declared these words to his inner core of disciples, those He mentored: "A new command I give you: Love one another. As I have loved you, so you must love one another. By this everyone will know that you are my disciples, if you love one another" (John 13:34–35 NIV). Jesus authoritatively suggested that His brightest and best leaders in every generation would figure out what distinguished His love from all others and mimic it. God's love is a foundational principle of the Christian faith. The grace of God that draws us, heals us, transforms us and empowers us is essentially God's love in work clothes.

That is why it is essential that we take a closer look at this subject. Until we understand the important role that love plays in our lives, we will never understand what God is doing in the world and we will never be fueled to achieve our unique purpose. A proper understanding of love will show us why God was willing to send His only Son to die for our sins. It will also help clarify God's plan for our families, churches, communities and, most important, for each man and woman. As children of God, we all derive our sense of inner peace and wholeness from the understanding and power of God's love working in our hearts and spirits.

*The grace of God that draws us, heals us, transforms us and empowers us is essentially God's love in work clothes.*

## Risking It All

Near the end of His earthly ministry, Jesus gave the people of that day a dire warning:

> O, Jerusalem, Jerusalem, the one who kills the prophets and stones those who are sent to her! How often I wanted to gather your children together, as a hen gathers her chicks under her wings, but you were not willing!
>
> *Matthew 23:37*

This is such a powerful statement, but what was Jesus saying? His words were intentionally dramatic; He wanted these men to understand what their nation was forfeiting—a moment of divine intervention and national destiny.

Jesus paired His warning of coming dark days with a description of His shepherding heart. He has the power to rescue an entire city, ethnic group, our geographic nation—if they cooperate with Him and avoid squandering His love and grace. He can protect, as a hen shields her little chicks. This feminine concept may scare today's theologians, but the hard-boiled fishermen/disciples immediately grasped the farming analogy. However, just as in our day, the leadership elite of Jerusalem were not willing to listen to their true Messiah.

Just two verses later we see Jesus sitting with His disciples on the Mount of Olives, looking out across the Kidron Valley at the high and stately walls of the great Jewish temple, with all of Jerusalem spread out in the distance. Undoubtedly, the young men, simple men—fishermen, carpenters, shepherds—were dazzled by the wealth and power of the Jewish capital. But then Jesus asked, "Do you not see all these things? Assuredly, I say to you, not one stone shall be left here upon another, that shall not be thrown down" (Matthew 24:2).

The disciples must have been astonished by His words. Had Jesus lost His mind? Jerusalem was a sprawling city, the most amazing place they had ever seen, the commercial and religious center of the entire region. Solomon's Temple, which had been destroyed by the Babylonians nearly six hundred years earlier, had been rebuilt bigger and grander than ever by King Herod. Those towers dominated the city and the culture. But over time the people's hearts had grown cold and their religion was all for show and for their own glory. In their vanity and false pride, the people no longer served

God or lived as the Scriptures demanded. So Jesus gave them a warning; but, predictably, the people refused to listen.

So what does this short passage say for us today? First, God has a plan for our lives. Second, only hungry and humble people seek Him (see Matthew 5:1–13). Third, it highlights the fact that only a small percentage of believers in any generation will develop a kingdom worldview. Consider Matthew 7:13 from three different translations:

> "Enter through the narrow gate. For wide is the gate and broad is the road that leads to destruction, and many enter through it." (NIV1984)

> "You can enter God's Kingdom only through the narrow gate. The highway to hell is broad, and its gate is wide for the many who choose that way." (NLT)

> "Enter by the narrow gate. For the gate is wide and the way is easy that leads to destruction, and those who enter by it are many." (ESV)

The fact that you are reading this book is a sign that you want to be right in the middle of God's purposes in this generation. I do, too! And not only does God have a plan for your life and mine, but there is strategic timing for the fulfillment of that plan.

## The Timing of Love

When the children of Israel left Egypt, they decided not to enter the Promised Land immediately. As they debated about the giants, the Lord deemed them unworthy of entry and announced His punishment upon them (see Numbers 14). The next day they decided to try to obey the Lord's original commandment—just one day late. Moses tried to explain that they had missed their moment, but the rebellious crowd went up to take the land anyway. As a result of missing the obedient season of response, the Amalekites and Canaanites from the hill country came down and defeated them easily (see Numbers 14:45). Just like arriving at a supermarket after the electronic doors have been turned off, we sometimes fail to receive entrance into our prepared destination.

The purpose of this book is to help you enter into your personal promised land—"the more" God has prepared for us. Timing is always key. If we are too late, we miss out and we have to wait for the next open door of opportunity. In the case of the former slaves leaving Israel the cycle of change was forty years. For us, spiritual lateness could cost us a decade of opportunity.

Over the years, like myriad others, including former President Clinton, I have had a problem with perennial lateness. I have learned that lateness is sometimes caused by laziness or an extreme lack of discipline. In my case, however, a time management expert explained that some people are habitually late because they are actually attempting to squeeze too much into one day. These folks must discipline themselves to limit the number of commitments and to make realistic assessments about what they can actually accomplish in 24 hours. I learned that having clear focused goals and copious amounts of unscheduled time is a kind of wealth, a wealth of purpose.

Management guru Stephen Covey described it as making sure our ladder is placed against the right wall. A good strategic plan and a schedule that has a lot of free time for rest, reflection and responding to the unexpected, will allow a person to be extraordinarily successful. When I say yes to a new vision, I also am saying yes to a set of responsibilities and appointments—if I am going to arrive at my destiny on time.

As I have thought deeply about applying the principles of daily planning to life and career planning, I have realized that many of us miss our destiny because we don't prioritize the "known will of God" enough. We often fail to trust the love and faithfulness of God. In an expression of unbelief, I have occasionally been guilty of hedging my bets. Jesus was clear as He taught His disciples the following truth: "If you love me, keep my commands. And I will ask the Father, and he will give you another advocate to help you and be with you forever—the Spirit of truth" (John 14:15–17 NIV).

> *Many of us miss our destiny because we don't prioritize the "known will of God" enough.*

Jesus said the world would know we are His disciples by our love. Our personal love for Christ must be turned into service. In a way, it is like a professional chauffeur who is willing to wait at the client's door until he is ready to go. Even if the client makes the chauffeur wait for a hour before beginning the journey, he waits with the understanding that he contracted to serve with a professional demeanor until his time is up. He is being paid handsomely to serve the client's agenda and timing. As he waits outside the client's home, he cannot judge the client's timing or agenda. He cannot get so bored or distracted that he forgets that he is not the star of the show. He has, however, been given the privilege of access and service. Likewise, I have learned that I can make a huge difference in the world, if I relentlessly serve the Master's agenda.

Persecution is an honor. Trouble and pressure become an honor (see Matthew 5:9–11) if I embrace the role of a servant. Solomon warns us in the Bible that even when it seems like "management" is set against us, we must not leave our assigned sphere of influence until He releases us from our post (see Ecclesiastes 10:1–4). Other people's needs and our fascinations with "shiny objects" cause many of us to miss seizing our moment of fruitfulness, blessing and favor.

## The Transforming Power of Love

God is love, and Jesus sacrificed His life for us because of His great love. Jesus taught us how to love one another, and nowhere is the relationship of love and trust more essential than in the family. One way or another, we are all part of a family. We were born into a family, and many of us have spouses and children; we are raising our own families, and this is good. God ordained that the family should be the glue that holds the culture together. As long as the family is strong and God is at the center of our lives, the culture will prosper. But if we ignore God's plan and, in our pride and arrogance, we decide to do everything our own way, we are inviting disaster.

Our challenge today is that many of us are broken stones with which God wants to build a strong structure. But know this: His healing grace can restore the broken places in us, which will allow the healing of fragmented families. It all begins with us receiving the healing power of grace and love. In Galatians 5:5–6, Paul explains that righteousness and Christian character manifest as a result of faith working by love. The Holy Spirit helps us end personal sin patterns. The process begins with the hope and expectation that come from experiencing conversion and the Father's love. We must believe first of all that we belong in the beloved community of grace (see Ephesians 1:6). Second, we are encouraged to have faith that we can be changed by the power of God. There is hope for the manipulator, the verbal abuser, the porn-addicted man to grow in Christ.

We change by recognizing our faults, repenting (having a change of heart and mind), receiving God's grace and working through the sometimes painful process of personal transformation. This is how I overcame my weight problems (caused by nervous eating) and lost 130 pounds in two years and kept them off. The desire to please God (a love response) teamed with a sense of God's acceptance of me as a son (His Agape or divine love) and gave me the inner motivation to keep fighting my "inner demons" and the downward pull of the flesh. This process is also how I

*It is important to follow God's plan for our lives rather than the trendy pronouncements of psychologists and pundits, even some preachers, who are pushing "fool's gold."*

walked out of a battle with negativity. It also helped me avoid falling into the trap of addiction to pornography, cigarettes and countless other snares.

And because I believe it is important to follow God's plan for our lives rather than the trendy pronouncements of psychologists and pundits, even some preachers, who are pushing "fool's gold," I not only want to offer you action steps to breakthroughs in your own life, but foundational keys that can make us wiser as individuals and more blessed as a nation.

If we take another look at Jesus' words to the men of Jerusalem, it is clear that He was speaking to the men and women of our day, as well.

O, Jerusalem, Jerusalem, the one who kills the prophets and stones those who are sent to her! How often I wanted to gather your children together, as a hen gathers her chicks under her wings, but you were not willing!

*Matthew 23:37*

Only someone who loves you deeply could speak such words, but there is deep sadness in what Jesus was saying. He says how often He wanted to gather His people together, to care for them, to teach them, to love and shelter them, but they were not willing to receive what He could give.

His words were first directed at the leaders of His day; secondly, at a carnal group of religious thrill-seekers who were tone deaf (they had no clue as to what He was saying); and thirdly, at true disciples who were going to walk with Him despite the nation destroying its spiritual legacy. These true believers were responsible for bringing us the Word. So

Jesus' breath was not wasted, even though there was so much more He would have liked to have achieved.

How tragic for the nation of Israel to reject their true Messiah, to miss out on the joy they could have experienced. We know what happened. History tells us that Jerusalem was destroyed by the Roman legions in the year AD 70, just one generation after Jesus spoke those words. In AD 135 every last inhabitant of that place was murdered or driven out by Hadrian's legions, and the people of that ancient land were scattered to the four winds. For eighteen long centuries Jerusalem remained a wasteland, until 1948 when at long last, as the prophet Ezekiel prophesied, those dry bones were brought back to life as the modern state of Israel.

When Jesus wept over Jerusalem, He knew what was coming, but His warning was rejected. In much the same way, the Bible gives us a dramatic warning of what happens when we fail to listen to God's Word.

## Your True Identity

I am convinced that many of the problems we face today are the result of individual believers never finding their true identity in God. Broken homes and broken families produce broken people who have lost their sense of identity. Too many mothers and fathers no longer understand who they are, and consequently they are raising boys and girls who are adrift on the stormy seas of a godless generation, looking for meaning, looking for a purpose and settling in many cases for the first thing that comes along that feels like a family. Does that sound familiar? Our personal identity often comes from whom we belong to—our family or tribe—or it can come from our accomplishments. The dramatic rise in teen suicide, promiscuity and drug abuse is due in part to a huge "father wound" in the lives of young people around the world. Our family and marital problems will be lessened if we could get dads back into their homes.

But now I want to tell you something else, and I hope this will be a blessing to you. Before Jesus began His ministry—at least three years before the passage above where He wept over the city of Jerusalem and spoke those prophetic words—He came face-to-face with this same question of identity. Even though Jesus had both an earthly father and a heavenly Father, He struggled with self-identity. Jesus, the Bible says, was tested as we are tested, and He had to ask Himself: Who am I? Why am I here? What is My purpose in life? And what does God want Me to do?

Our true identity must be anchored in the Word of God. This means Scripture reading, memorization and renewing my mind with God's perspective of my role and duties. All this is imperative to walking in freedom. I shock congregations when I declare, "I used to be black; then I became a Christian." I simply mean that my faith defines me most decisively.

Matthew's gospel tells us that immediately after Jesus was baptized by John the Baptist and the Holy Spirit lighted on Him like a dove, Jesus was led out into the wilderness to be tested by the devil. This was a test to see if He was truly committed to His assignment. The passage tells us that Jesus was in the desert for nearly six weeks without eating anything. It must have been painful, but He continued fasting and praying, in communion with the Father.

But seeing that Jesus was in a physically weakened condition—this is how the devil usually operates—Satan came at Jesus like an old fox, to challenge Him and tempt Him to lose focus. He said, "If You are the Son of God, command that these stones become bread." Jesus could have ordered up a seven-course meal any time He wanted to, but He knew what was going on, and He wasn't about to give in to the devil. He said, "It is written, 'Man shall not live by bread alone, but by every word that proceeds from the mouth of God.'"

Jesus won round one without a fight, but the battle wasn't over. Matthew tells us,

> Then the devil took Him up into the holy city, set Him on the pinnacle of the temple, and said to Him, "If You are the Son of God, throw Yourself down. For it is written: 'He shall give His angels charge over you,' and, 'In their hands they shall bear you up, Lest you dash your foot against a stone.'"

I can just imagine the scowl on Jesus' face when He answered, "It is written again, 'You shall not tempt the LORD your God.'"

Satan must have known he was defeated, but he came back a third time to break the Lord's resolve. Matthew writes,

> Again, the devil took Him up on an exceedingly high mountain, and showed Him all the kingdoms of the world and their glory. And he said to Him, "All these things I will give You if You will fall down and worship me."

By this time Jesus had had enough, and He turned on that old snake and said, "Away with you, Satan! For it is written, 'You shall worship the LORD your God, and Him only you shall serve.'" Then, knowing it was a good time to make a speedy exit, the devil left Him, and I love what Matthew says next: "Behold, angels came and ministered to Him" (Matthew 3:16–4:11).

Because Jesus was faithful to His calling, rejecting every temptation of the enemy, God sent angels to bring Him food and water, and they ministered to His spirit. This is a wonderful story for many reasons, but what leaps out from the pages is the fact that Jesus knew who He was. He knew His true identity, and He was not about to fall for the lies and empty promises of the devil.

But here is what I hope you will remember: If you know who you are, then you can do whatever your assignment is. If you know who you are and where you belong, you can walk with confidence as a child of the King. But if you do not know who you are, you will never have the confidence to do what you have been called to do. No matter how much potential you have, you will be stymied by doubt and indecision. Lacking a grasp of your true identity, Satan will have an easy time with you.

When Satan came after Jesus, his goal was to shatter the sense of connection between Jesus and the Father. But Jesus said, "Get behind Me, Satan!" He was not about to let that happen. And do you see how He defeated the devil? Coming face-to-face with the enemy, Jesus quotes Scripture to him. Now, it may be that two of those times Jesus was reminding

Himself of the protocol of the kingdom (the rules and regulations); but the third time, He was doing business, and He said with all the passion and authority of the Son of God, "Away with you, Satan!"

This is a powerful lesson about the reality of spiritual warfare. From time to time we hear people talking about wrestling with the devil, putting on the full armor of God or the kind of faith we need to fend off "the fiery darts of the wicked one," but you need to understand that the attacks of Satan will not always be so easy to spot. The devil almost always comes after you at the point of your greatest weakness. For Jesus, it was at the end of a forty-day fast when He was hungry and thirsty; for you and me, it may be something much simpler, sometime when it is much easier to give in, sometime when we are the most vulnerable.

But regardless how or when the tempter comes, if we take the approach that Jesus took, we are going to stay on our assignment; we are not going to be distracted. We are going to stay faithful to what we have been called to do. Our obedience is an expression of worship and fidelity, and as long as Jesus remained on His assignment, miracles would happen, because He was the Messiah. And as long as we remain faithful to do what the Father has called us to do, miracles will happen, because we have been redeemed by the Son of God and called to His service. If we get distracted, however, we will find ourselves in the wrong place at the wrong time, and the mission will become uncertain. The people we were sent to will not be touched.

The first work of the enemy is simply to get us distracted by questioning our assignment and tempting us with other things. He wants to stir up an attitude of arrogance and presumption, tempting us to do things in our own strength rather than keeping our focus on the authority and power of the Holy Spirit. Jesus said, "If you love Me, you will keep My commandments." So the impetus for personal holiness really is love, which brings us back to where we started.

This is so important, because if we truly love God, we will remain faithful to the calling He has placed on our lives, and He will give us a sense of destiny. And if we are tied to our identity, we can know God's purpose for our lives. We are not just an afterthought with some random assignment somewhere in the universe. God loves us with an everlasting love, and there is a specific place where we have been called to serve. Scripture says we are fearfully and wonderfully made (see Psalm 139:14). God knew us before we were in our mother's womb, and if we have given our hearts to Jesus Christ, we can be sure we have a destiny. And if we want to please the Redeemer of our souls, it should be easy for us to respond by keeping His commandments.

> *And as long as we remain faithful to do what the Father has called us to do, miracles will happen.*

Whenever persecution and temptation come along, as they certainly will, we should not be surprised. We are in the midst of a spiritual war, and the stakes could not be higher, and that is why we need to be fully grounded in the Word of God. Paul writes,

> Who shall separate us from the love of Christ? Shall tribulation, or distress, or persecution, or famine, or nakedness, or

peril, or sword? As it is written: "For Your sake we are killed all day long; we are accounted as sheep for the slaughter." Yet in all these things we are more than conquerors through Him who loved us.

*Romans 8:35–37*

Christ has already given us the resources we need to overcome trials and tribulation. The Greek word translated *tribulation* simply means "pressure." That the Lord will deliver us from grinding, personal pressure is a huge promise. For me the pressure of financial deadlines in an atmosphere of diminishing resources has been the place where I have been tested the most. But Paul goes on to say,

For I am persuaded that neither death nor life, nor angels nor principalities nor powers, nor things present nor things to come, nor height nor depth, nor any other created thing, shall be able to separate us from the love of God which is in Christ Jesus our Lord.

*verses 38–39*

The idea is that all these things are going to try to separate us from Christ's love. So we should know beforehand that this will be part of the package. The enemy does not want us to fulfill our calling, and he is working overtime to undermine our effectiveness.

But let me tell you something else. If you want to know where Satan will attack, here are six areas: your humility, trust, love, faithfulness, endurance and purity. There may be others as well, but we are focusing on these areas in this work. I believe they are at the top of Satan's list of targets because they are at the top of God's list of priorities for your life and your ministry as a follower of Jesus Christ.

At one time or another, all of us are going to have opportunities to give up on the call of God. To resist the wiles of the devil, we have to be anchored in love, and we need to see the crisis we are in, whatever it may be, as an opportunity to follow this awakened understanding that there is a way out. God is going to lay out a path of love and obedience. If we are walking intimately with the Lord, we will find ourselves on a pathway out of adversity. We will be able to fight our way through temptation and persecution—refined, purified and more productive than ever. But it only works if we are anchored in the identity of love and acceptance, and that means understanding our role in the family of God.

# 4

# MORE THAN CONQUERORS

*Step Four: Endure in the Face of Adversity*

*M*aybe you have already come face-to-face with this reality, but the secular world wants nothing to do with your religious beliefs. Thanks to decades of relative peace and comfort, a lot of moral confusion and a lot of misinformation, they have chosen the path that says "to thine own self be true." The names of Jesus and God are only curse words for some of these folks, and the church of Jesus Christ is an object of scorn. As the Bible says, their god is their belly and their glory is in their shame. They have set their minds on earthly things, and Scripture warns that their end will be destruction (see Philippians 3:19).

Oh yes, even the most irreligious man or woman may admit from time to time that there is something out there. Even the most hardhearted atheist will occasionally experience a God-ward impulse. There is a reason for that. Paul writes, "Since the creation of the world His invisible attributes are clearly seen, being understood by the things that are made" (Romans 1:20). The creation is all the proof we need of a Creator, but today's secular-minded society does not want to know about God. They do not want to admit they are sinners, and they do not want to make the difficult lifestyle choices God would demand of them. That is why they are so quick to deny your religious freedom, trying to shut you down.

So how is the Christian supposed to remain strong in the face of such hostility? How can we expect to experience genuine transformation when the world wants nothing to do with what God has to say? And how can we be witnesses for our faith in such a hardened world? Once again, the answer comes from Scripture, where we are encouraged repeatedly to persevere in doing good. Writing in Galatians, Paul says, "Let us not grow weary while doing good, for in due season we shall reap if we do not lose heart" (Galatians 6:9). And the writer of Hebrews adds, "Let us lay aside every weight, and the sin which so easily ensnares us, and let us run with endurance the race that is set before us" (Hebrews 12:1).

As in every important endeavor, true success comes through endurance and perseverance. It may not be easy, and it may cost you the friendship of someone you admire. But if you pursue goals you know to be true and good with endurance and strength of purpose, you will not be disappointed. Every step you take toward transformation and spiritual maturity will bring you closer to the success God has planned for you. Yes, there will be challenges along the way, and there may even be persecution. But as the apostle Paul assures us, "In all these things we are more than conquerors through Him who loved us" (Romans 8:37).

One of the greatest blessings of my life has been to serve a congregation of deeply committed Christians in the nation's capital district. From our home base in south central Maryland, we have been blessed to touch the lives of tens of thousands of men, women and children in one of the most dynamic and influential parts of the country. Through our outreach efforts, special programs and the gospel preaching that is central to everything we do, our church is helping to change the atmosphere in our city.

*Whoever you are, wherever you live and whatever you do, God can use you to help transform the atmosphere around you.*

But something else is happening as well. A shift is taking place. Since we began lifting our voices in the city, there is a growing sensitivity to the righteousness and justice for which we stand. I believe our church as a whole is living out this message, and you can too. Whoever you are, wherever you live and whatever you do, God can use you to help transform the atmosphere around you. Wherever the Spirit of the Lord is found there is a fragrance of divine grace that permeates the very air we breathe.

But let me give you a little more mundane example. Have you ever gone into someone's home for a visit, and as soon as you walk through the door you know exactly what they had for dinner? The smell is heavy and unpleasant and just hangs in the air. You can deal with it, but it is not a pleasant experience. Well, that happens at my house every now and then. You see, I am not a fish lover. I do not eat much fish, but my family just loves it. So sometimes when I have to go out of town my wife and daughters conspire against me! They get together and cook up a bunch of fish. Okay. That's fine. I am glad they enjoy it, and I am especially glad when they finish everything before I get home.

The problem is, when I get home I can still smell the fish, so I immediately make for the closet where we keep the air freshener, and before long I can breathe again. Today we are blessed to have time-released air fresheners. You know what I mean? You can take these little pods and put them up on the wall and they spray once every minute or two, putting out a wonderful aroma. Those things are very useful when I come home. But there are times when the unpleasant odors we encounter are not as simple as somebody's last meal. Sometimes the only thing that can make our lives bearable is the fresh aroma of God's time-released grace, perfuming and renewing the air around us.

The Spirit of the Lord says, "Behold, I make all things new" (Revelation 21:5). What a blessing that can be when you find yourself in an environment where there are sounds or smells that are unpleasant and offensive. Maybe you have been struggling with the atmosphere in the workplace, where you are surrounded by vulgar and offensive language all the time. For others it may be a problem in your neighborhood, or perhaps in your home. The world exudes a very different odor, doesn't it?

Unfortunately, we can't always change things right away when our faith-based sensibilities are offended. But the good news is that God has given each of us the ability to change the atmosphere around us by His grace. In some ways it is like that air freshener on the wall. The process begins with prayer. Scripture says, "The effective, fervent prayer of a righteous man avails much" (James 5:16). Change doesn't always happen overnight, and patience really is a virtue. But prayer and a quiet, faithful witness can work miracles. It is as if God is saying, Just hit that button and change the atmosphere around you by the grace that I have released into your life.

## Your Spiritual Breakthrough

Are you ready for an extreme makeover in your life? Maybe you feel stuck in your job. Maybe you are thinking you need to move on to something else, but that can be hard to do. You may feel that you are not appreciated where you are today. Nobody really cares about what is going on in your life at home or on the job. These are certainly issues you ought to be concerned about. But what if the problem is not with them but with you? What if the problem is that you are not taking advantage of the resources that Christ has already given you?

If you want to be a catalyst for change—that is, if you want to be the kind of person who can call upon the grace of God to make dramatic changes in your environment—one of the first things you will have to do is to break the cycle of crying, "Woe is me!" Feeling sorry for yourself will get you nowhere. You have got to lose the feeling that you are not going to make it.

Don't get me wrong—life is NOT fair! And it is not just the folks at the bottom who feel like giving up. Some ministers have "slipped" into adultery or drugs as their own way of committing "spiritual suicide" by police. "Suicide by police" is the act of taking one's own life by intentionally provoking a lethal response from a law officer. Consider, for example, former policeman Christopher Dorner, who in February 2013 wrote a manifesto and declared war on the system. He felt used. He was bitter. He knew that if he broke the rules, he would go out in a blaze of glory. He would not have to think about being a "hero" again. Sometimes promising Christian leaders commit "spiritual suicide" so they don't have to serve God in the painful hidden years, as Moses did on the back side of the desert.

This is equally true for those who are business owners and top-level managers. You have got to put aside the thought that if you only had more money or more people or more time (or whatever you are blaming for your unhappiness), you could achieve your goals. Those are just excuses. You already have everything you need to accomplish your goals. What you need now is a spiritual breakthrough.

Earlier I mentioned that the Chinese word for *crisis* is made up of two characters related to danger and opportunity. Nobody wants to get caught in the middle of a crisis, but the fact is, finding yourself in a crisis situation could be the doorway to a new opportunity. You may remember when a White House staffer made the comment a few years ago, "Never let a good crisis go to waste." It seemed like such a cynical remark at the time, but if you trust in the grace of God to transform your situation, what looks like a crisis today may be just the opportunity you have been praying for.

*If you want to be a catalyst for change . . . break the cycle of crying, "Woe is me!"*

As we have already seen, God offers us four dimensions of grace. If we do not frustrate His grace, and if we are prepared to receive His grace at each level, Christ will move us out of the areas of crisis in our lives into the spiritual breakthrough we have been praying for. We can come out of the wilderness into the Promised Land if we are willing to embrace the grace of God.

The kind of grace I am talking about is progressive. In other words, it comes in waves. God wants us to make a difference, to be a catalyst for change. He wants us to change the atmosphere where we live. But if we do not understand and embrace the waves of grace He offers us, we will just continue to wallow around in the same old problems, stuck in disappointment and failure. But God has provided four dimensions of grace, and we become part of His plan of transformation when we accept the grace He has provided.

Earlier I used a metaphor of survival grace as protection in an automobile accident. In a situation like that you do not have time to go off and fast for three days and seek deliverance from the wreck that is about to happen. Survival grace is a demonstration of the unmerited favor of God. It comes when a car crosses the yellow line and hits you head-on, and the EMTs are saying there is no hope for you. They bring the Jaws of Life and cut the car open; then they strap you to a gurney and move you ever so gently to the ambulance because they believe your neck may be broken. But what they do not know is that you are surrounded by God's survival grace. By the time you arrive at the hospital the emergency team discovers that the only thing wrong with you is a bad bruise.

Survival grace may also be miraculously provided when your doctor orders a series of tests and says you have a 10 percent chance of survival. But as you start getting treatment, you suddenly begin feeling better. Then one day the folks in the rehabilitation center wonder why you are there, because you do not look sick anymore. This actually happened to one of my daughters.

Survival grace is when you haven't had time to say or do anything to engage your faith but the protective hand of God is upon you, and you come through that crisis because of His grace. The problem we can have with this kind of grace is that we may be tempted to complain about the situation we are in instead of praising God with joy and thanksgiving, recognizing what the Lord has done for us.

*Once I recognized that God had imparted a measure of grace to me, my thinking shifted.*

When I was going through the worst of my bout with cancer, some folks were telling me, "I know you're scared,

Harry. But you don't need to worry." Actually, I wasn't scared. I was living under a dispensation of faith. I am not saying my faith in the normal realm was all that great, and I complained quite a bit at first. But what happened sometime early on in the process was that supernatural faith kicked in. When I was diagnosed with cancer, everybody I spoke to told me about relatives or friends who were diagnosed with cancer of the esophagus and died within weeks of the diagnosis. Yet, somehow, by the grace of God I was still alive! Once I recognized that God had imparted a measure of grace to me, my thinking shifted. I stopped complaining. I thanked Him for His mercy, and I acknowledged that His grace was sufficient for me.

## Oh, Taste and See

Some folks who are unhappy in the workplace don't realize that still being in their current job is a miracle. Some unhappy business owners don't realize that just keeping the doors of that business open so they can earn a living and serve the community is a demonstration of God's grace. Some of us aren't aware that God has already tempered the attack of the enemy and is holding us in His grace. His grace is already working, but unless you take time to express your gratitude to God for what He is doing in your life, you may not be able to see how truly blessed you are.

We all know how to look a gift horse in the mouth, don't we? We are pretty good at grumbling and complaining even when things are going along pretty well. The psalmist says,

"Oh, taste and see that the LORD is good; blessed is the man who trusts in Him!" (Psalm 34:8). But too often we are more like the Israelites who were murmuring and complaining when God was bringing them out of the wilderness. And all that murmuring just made their problems worse.

They did not obey God because they did not understand His ways or trust Him to do what He said He would do. As a result, they wandered in the wilderness for forty years. They brought all that suffering on themselves because of a lack of trust in the protective, preserving hand of God. If they had just done what He said, the Israelites would have been fine. But they were preoccupied with their own petty interests, and their murmuring compounded the judgments of God upon them.

They were already being judged with forty years of wandering, but in the middle of that sentence they started complaining about what they didn't have to eat. They were in that predicament because of sin and their refusal to trust in the wisdom of God and His appointed leaders, but they were blaming God for what they had done to themselves. In the long run they suffered because they would not give God thanks for what they did have. You see, there is a way of deliverance from our troubles, but the breakthrough begins by being thankful for God's provision regardless of the predicament you may be in.

Do you remember the words of the great hymn "Great Is Thy Faithfulness"? It is one of the most memorable songs recorded by the great gospel singer Larnell Harris. The words come from the book of Lamentations: "Through the LORD's mercies we are not consumed, because His compassions fail not. They are new every morning; great is Your faithfulness" (3:22–23). We will never understand God's ways. His ways are above our ways, but we know that He will always keep His promises; He will always be faithful to us; and regardless of the struggles we may be facing, we ought to be grateful for His faithfulness, declaring that His mercies are new every morning.

This is just as true in the workplace as it is in the church on Sunday morning, or in your personal life. Those of you who are married with children need to thank God for the family God has given you. They are your treasure, and He wants to bless you through your family. Those of you who are single, praying for the right person to come into your life, need to be thankful for God's mercy, knowing that He has a plan for each and every life. Those who have the money to pay the rent should be grateful for His provision, knowing that we are dependent on His bounty.

Actually, most of us live well beyond our means these days. We eat too well, we spend too much money. Some folks are taking trips to exotic destinations and making improvements on their already comfortable homes, and most of the time they are still not satisfied, still wanting more. By the grace of God we are not living in the grinding poverty that many people in the world are forced to endure, but how often do we stop to thank God for that? If you pause for even a second I am sure you can think of many, many things to be thankful for, and these are all reasons to praise God and thank Him for His mercy. But let me tell you something very important: Praising God releases the flow of grace into your life.

Before I get too carried away, let me acknowledge that there are people in every community who find themselves in desperate circumstances from time to time. I found myself on my back in the hospital, being treated by an oncologist, and many people had apparently decided my time was up. I didn't *have* to survive; there was nothing automatic about it. And, trust me, being a pastor doesn't give you any special exemption from the trials and tribulations of life. It may give you a reservoir of experience, but God did not have to spare my life. He did not have to stay the hand of the avenger who was trying to kill me. But in His mercy and grace, God let me live.

*Praising God releases the flow of grace into your life.*

I know, however, that some of us are barely holding on, barely able to keep our jobs, barely able to hold on to our homes, barely able to deal with our children who are being tempted by the false promises of the secular world. But despite all the difficulties you face, you are still holding on. You need to be thankful you are able to write that check and pay your bills. You may not know where the money will come from next month, but you can be thankful for what you have.

If we begin with thankfulness, we will see God's grace come to bear. Wallowing in anger, doubt and negativity prevents us from entering into a relationship with God. A defeatist attitude about the natural world around you will keep you from participating in the supernatural blessings that God has prepared for His children. The apostle Paul assures us, "Eye has not seen, nor ear heard, nor have entered into the heart of man the things which God has prepared for those who love Him" (1 Corinthians 2:9). We see it over and over throughout the Scriptures: God is looking for ways to bless His children. But He reserves His blessings for those who are faithful and who are content to rely upon His mercy and grace.

God just wants you to push the grace buttons. It is a bit like the Easy button on the Staples TV commercials. You have your own easy button that releases the grace of God into your life, and it is right in front of you. If you have truly placed your trust in Him, there is no reason not to push that button.

## He Cares for You

In the book of Job, we read the story of a man who has lived a good and godly life. At one time he had a large and prosperous family, and the Bible tells us Job was faithful to observe all the commandments of the Lord. Although he did his best to honor God in everything, his family is slaughtered, his children are murdered and all his crops and animals are wiped out. Suddenly this man who had been one of the richest men of his day lost everything. To make matters worse, he is suddenly covered with boils and sores that won't heal. There can hardly be a worse combination of horrors, and Job is afraid he has been cursed by God.

What Job doesn't know, however, is that God has allowed him to be tested, not because he has done great evil, but because he has done so much good. When Satan says that

Job is only faithful to God because of all the blessings he has received, God allows the devil to push Job to the limit. In the midst of his troubles, Job cries out,

> He has made me a byword of the people, and I have become one in whose face men spit. My eye has also grown dim because of sorrow, and all my members [meaning every part of his body] are like shadows. Upright men are astonished at this, and the innocent stirs himself up against the hypocrite.
>
> *Job 17:6–8*

There is no doubt Job had good reasons to complain about his situation. But the amazing thing is that after telling us all about his sorrows and tribulations, he begins to speak about how he knows that God watches over the steps of the righteous. Despite his suffering, Job expresses his firm belief that those who place their trust in God will come through their trials even stronger than before. This is such an important lesson for every one of us today.

Job says, "Though He slay me, yet will I trust Him," and he adds, "He also shall be my salvation" (Job 13:15–16). If you have read the rest of this story, you know how it turns out. Job was right about God's faithfulness. In the end, Satan is confounded by Job's perseverance. In the depth of his misery, Job's wife had urged him to "curse God and die" (Job 2:9). She thought death would be better than the torture her husband was enduring. But Job does not turn against God, and despite the worst that Satan could do to him, his faith only grows stronger. Then, as a sign of God's favor for this faithful man, Job's family, his crops and animals and his wealth are all restored, greater than he had before.

The reason the Bible is full of such stories is to assure us that God is faithful. No matter how deep the pit we have fallen into, and no matter how much the world may scoff at our beliefs, God is faithful. He has answers for all who call upon His name. He says, "I will never leave you nor forsake you" (Hebrews 13:5). His resources are greater than anything we can imagine, and all He asks is that we remain humble and faithful, trusting Him to supply our needs, even in the darkest times. All of which brings me to three important principles of the extreme makeover He offers us.

First of all, you need to know that God is with you everywhere and at all times, and He can be trusted. We all go through hard times; it is just part of life. But knowing that we have a loving and merciful God who will never leave us or forsake us ought to fill our hearts with joy. At the end of the tiny New Testament book of Jude, we find a short prayer that has been used for centuries as a benediction, reminding generations of believers that God "is able to keep you from stumbling, and to present you faultless before the presence of His glory with exceeding joy" (Jude 24).

When you read those words and discover that God is able to keep you from stumbling, wouldn't you say that is an example of divine grace? This kind of grace is protective and preventative. The security we have in our faith is based on knowing that we have a God who is able to keep us from falling and to present us faultless, even on the day of judgment, kneeling before the throne of God. These words ought to fill every heart with joy. Job understood what Jude was saying, and Paul understood as well, not in spite of the suffering and hardship they had endured, but because of it. The crisis situations they faced taught them that God is faithful and true in every circumstance. Despite the dangers they faced, they discovered new opportunities to grow in grace.

Second, we need to know that God is at work in our character whenever we are going through hard times, whether it is a family problem, a career problem or something else. Remember, God may be keeping you in that place because there is something He is trying to accomplish—either in you or in those around you. He wants to present you faultless before the presence of His glory, and that could mean that you will have to undergo some type of hardship to prepare you for the journey.

## Taking the Heat

Faultlessness is a character trait. To be faultless has to do with being more like Jesus. It means that you are being prepared to stand before a holy God one day "without blame." To be faultless means you can be trusted to act in an honorable and responsible way, with honesty, integrity and a spirit of servanthood. Unfortunately, some folks head off to their jobs each day thinking they are entitled to do whatever they like. They think the company owes them a living, so they demand to be treated in a certain way. But they don't feel the same sense of obligation to their employer. Too many are more concerned with their "rights" than with their "responsibilities."

The state of Maryland, where I live and work, is a right-to-work state. This means that, if the company happens to be unionized, each employee has the right to decide whether or not they want to be a member of the union. But it also means that the employer can fire an under-performing employee without having to go through arbitration. Raises are earned based on how well the employee performs his or her job, but if an employee is not performing up to a certain standard, or if the company simply cannot afford to keep that person on the payroll any longer, the employee can be terminated at any time.

When I was a boy, I used to hear the expression, "Nobody owes you a living." A lot of people today would be inclined to disagree with that statement, but I happen to believe it is still true. If you have a job, it is because your employer thought you could do something to help that company be more successful. The company pays you for your service, not because you are such a wonderful person, but because you do a job they need done. Each employee deserves to be respected and treated fairly, but we also need to have the attitude when we go to work that we are there to serve, to lift the company up, to help increase profits.

I wonder how many of us have ever prayed for a breakthrough for our company. The fact is, whenever a company fails, the employees fail right along with it. But when the company succeeds, the employees are part of the success, and they ought to be grateful for that. Maybe God is calling you to fast and pray for your company, for your fellow employees or for your supervisors. "Lord, it seems like things are out of control around here. My boss is stressed out and maybe that is why she is behaving that way, because she is under so much pressure. So God, please release Your mercy upon this company and my co-workers." I think God would welcome a prayer like that.

The point is, sometimes the change we are praying for may need to start with a change in us. It could be that Jesus has placed us in a job with troublesome people so that old "Mr. Sandpaper," who has been giving us such a hard time, can rub off some of our rough edges. I love what Bishop Wellington Boone said on one occasion about dealing with hardship. He said that God will "grow up" His people by "revelation or tribulation." He meant that if someone responds to the illuminated word and obeys new scriptural insights as soon as they come, he grows the easy way. Others, like children in old-fashioned classrooms, resist change and have the "board of education applied to their seat of understanding." Another slant on "revelation or tribulation" is that the Lord will allow us to keep stumbling at a task until we understand that our methods are antiquated and no longer sanctioned by God. But if that doesn't do it, God will find some other way to get us into shape.

Some circumstantial problems or hassles in our lives, which seem like persecution or spiritual warfare to us, may actually be God's providence grace or survival grace—keeping us out of much bigger trouble than we are able to imagine. Remember, God uses both "open doors" of divine opportunity and "closed doors" of divinely delayed opportunity to His glory (see Revelation 3:8–10). A final angle on the "revelation or tribulation" concept is this. You may be getting a little "ministry" on the job or from that irritating deacon at church. Your co-workers or your boss may be helping to apply a little pressure so that God can bring you into the place where you are being conformed to the image of Christ. If that rings a bell with you, you need to understand that when you are experiencing all those pressures, God is actually doing a magnificent work in you.

Trust me, I know what it feels like when God allows you to fight battles with a dual purpose. First, you advance His cause. Second, you are being changed progressively into His image. The ground game is your job. Character refinement is His job. Daily reading, daily prayer and communion with the Lord in worship is key.

> *Sometimes the change we are praying for may need to start with a change in us.*

From late 2004 (a year before the surgery and recovery stories outlined in this book) until late 2009, my family and I went through many severe battles that caused us to grow in both faith and character. I will share just one of my ordeals with you.

Our church had discovered a Christian day-care ministry next door to a new worship facility we had just purchased in 2004. After several months of prayer and negotiation, we put $350,000 of earnest money down on the purchase of this day-care facility. Our bank also gave us a commitment letter for the balance of the money needed to consummate the purchase. At the time, we owned several properties in the Washington, D.C., area; we also had a high-profile commercial tenant leasing a significant portion of one of our locations. Further, an 87-acre farm we owned was poised to sell for a huge profit that would fuel future ministry, enable the remodeling of our new headquarters and generally move us into a new level of both prestige and ministry effectiveness. As an individual, I was sitting on top of the world. As a ministry, we were there!

Unfortunately in late 2005, everything shifted suddenly. Cancer hit, the bottom fell out of the real estate market and I could not promote a major book I had written (*The Way of the Warrior*). More specifically, we could not close on the day-care deal. Our bank backed out of the deal due to the significant changes in both the market and our status. We lost the high-profile tenant, the contracted purchaser of the farm asked for a significant delay and our church tithes began to lag. I went from appearing like Abraham at his peak to looking like Job at his lowest. The day-care property was put into an auction process and our church was given the choice of losing the $350,000 outright or applying that money to a new bid.

At the end of a six-month process, the auctioneers asked the top four bidders to an office building in Baltimore. Each one of us had to bring a cashier's check, bank routing numbers or a way of closing the deal that day. My elders and I were extremely excited by the possibilities of winning the bid and not forfeiting the church's money. Unfortunately, two faith organizations were ahead of us in terms of the bids that we heard were set up by them. To complicate matters, the auctioneers warned us that we could not talk to the other bidders and promise side deals. As a result, I agonized over the deal. We had a clear financial limit.

The day of the closing, we showed up early with the largest multimillion dollar cashier's check I had ever seen. And yet we were in third place. The auctioneers went into the room of the highest bidder. To my team's shock, the highest bidder presented the auctioneers with a bank commitment letter that is legally binding for the bank for ninety days. This was a great strategy, but the auctioneers did not take it. At bidder number two's office, they received an offer considerably lower than what had been intimated to the auctioneer that they would be giving—so the auctioneer came to us. We produced the monetary instruments and won the bid for the property. Later I learned that one of the competing bidders, a pastor, was awakened out of his sleep by a disturbing dream, similar to Genesis 20:1–5, in which God told King Abimelech that he was as good as dead because he had designs on Abraham's wife. The pastor said that in a dream he heard these words: "If you steal Harry Jackson's property, things will not go well for you." Therefore, he did not aggressively pursue the bid. In this case, I had to remember that my congregation and I had a personal covenant with God concerning that land. Even though the nation had just moved into a severe recession and the real estate markets were unpredictable, the Lord delivered us from Satan's grip. God was also taking me to a deeper place of trust in Him just before I would have to trust Him with my entire life.

The psalmist said, "You prepare a table before me in the presence of my enemies" (Psalm 23:5). Sometimes God will deliver us while our enemies are watching, and while they have just enough space to swing but not to hit us. In those times we must learn how to stay calm and be absolutely at peace, because the devil, no matter how hard he tries, can't lay a glove on us.

In this story I see the entire four dimensions of transformational grace working in my congregation an extreme financial makeover:

Survival grace (providence)

Visionary grace (empowerment of the Holy Spirit)

Transitional grace (a personal covenant)

Establishment grace (sanctification)

Imagine going through a problem like the one I just described against the backdrop of an impending cancer surgery. It was easy to feel a lot of pressure and a strong sense of inadequacy. Once I realized the source of these feelings and corresponding sense of pressure, I started to relax and I began to rest in the strength of the Lord.

## Time to Turn Northward

One of the most important principles we learn at such times is that God is committed to us. But you may ask, how is God committed to us? Take another look at Jude 25, which says, "To God our Savior, who alone is wise, be glory and majesty, dominion and power, both now and forever." Through words of praise and benediction, Jude is assuring us of the wisdom and glory of our heavenly Father, who will reign forever, not only in His heavenly kingdom but here on earth, which is His earthly kingdom.

The word *kingdom* brings together two concepts, the king and his domain. The kingdom is the king's domain. Once we are saved by the blood of Jesus and begin walking in the light of the Word, we are living in the King's domain. The church is not God's only kingdom. Even when we walk outside the walls of the church, we are still living in the King's domain. He is in charge. He watches over His kingdom, and He has the final authority to say "Yay" or "Nay" to our requests. His domain and His rule supersede the rule of all earthly kings and rulers. His laws are higher than all our human laws. His provision is greater than any natural resources to which we have access. Furthermore, as subjects of an eternal kingdom, we have access to the power of a great and mighty King.

This means we are living with the capability of transforming our lives and our world by the power of the King's command. Do you see what an incredible blessing this is? As we speak out, live out and act out our lives in obedience to Him, He is not considering whether or not He is going to back us up. He is not wondering if He is going to bless us. He has already committed His power to us, and when we serve Him in humility, trust and love, calling upon His daily supply of strength and courage to help us face life's challenges, He empowers us to overcome the strongholds that are holding us back.

Suddenly the words of Jude 24–25 take on new meaning:

Now to Him who is able to keep you from stumbling, and to present you faultless before the presence of His glory with exceeding joy, to God our Savior, who alone is wise, be glory and majesty, dominion and power, both now and forever. Amen.

Isn't that powerful? He is saying that the way the King of glory is going to keep you from falling comes through a process that will help you to look and act more like Jesus.

You are going to know how to overcome the trials and tribulations that have kept you up nights and made you uncomfortable at your workplace. You will know something is happening when you begin to feel the joy bubbling up inside you in the midst of the storm. You will know that you have overcome the adversary when you begin to smile again. God has already done the heavy lifting, and you are going to come through that dark night, whatever the adversity may be, with a smile on our face.

> *God empowers us to overcome the strongholds that are holding us back.*

What I have learned through my own bouts of adversity and persecution is that God is doing powerful things in our lives. Just as He worked miracles for the ancient Israelites, He is working miracles in our lives today. The story of Moses and the twelve tribes of Israel wandering for forty years in the desert is a powerful example of God's provision. But I am especially struck by the remarkable words of Moses in Deuteronomy 2:

Then we turned and journeyed into the wilderness of the Way of the Red Sea, as the Lord spoke to me, and we skirted

Mount Seir for many days. And the LORD spoke to me, saying: "You have skirted this mountain long enough; turn
northward."

*verses 1–3*

Moses and the children of Israel were destined to shuffle
along in the wilderness for 40 years. That is a very long time
for anyone to travel with no idea of how to get to where they
are going. Nevertheless, at year 38, this multitude of sad and
weary travelers is coming back around again on an eleven-day
journey that has taken them 38 years to complete. By this
time they have probably memorized every rock, shrub and
rabbit hole—everything is looking way too familiar. Then,
suddenly, Moses hears the voice of the Lord speaking to him
with a surprising message.

It was something Moses had not heard for 38 years. The
Israelites were in distress. God had been in the midst of their
struggles all along. He had delivered them from disaster repeatedly, fed and protected them repeatedly and shown them
miracle after miracle. They had been given one demonstration
after another of God's survival grace, but they were not satisfied. They never seemed to get it. They must have felt as if
they were stuck in a holding pattern, but all this time God
was accomplishing a work in their lives. He was preparing
them for what was coming next.

Though God only communicated with them when it was
absolutely necessary, He had been there the whole time. But
suddenly He spoke to Moses and told him the Israelites were
nearing the end of their journey. With an audible voice, God

gave Moses these instructions. He said, "You have skirted this mountain long enough; turn northward."

Perhaps this is a word you need to hear as well. You have been struggling with your doubts and fears a very long time. But, in fact, you have everything you need. You serve a King whose power is unlimited; He has made His grace available to you and assured you that we are more than conquerors through Him who loves us. Still, you have prayed, you have complained and you are just doing the same old things, waiting for that miracle. But God says, *My dear child, you have skirted that mountain long enough. It is time to change directions.*

As I said at the beginning of this book, to find your way out of the wilderness you may have to turn around and go in a new direction. I believe that is what God is saying now. Do not let your doubts and discouragements hold you back any longer. You were born for more, but to experience all that He has planned for you, you need to place your life in His loving hands, praise Him and rest in His mercy and grace. Then take what you have learned and turn northward, toward the victory God had prepared for you all along.

# 5

# WHEN EVERYTHING CHANGES

*Step Five: Remain Faithful Even in Uncertain Times*

*I*f you are like me, it is hard to remember a time when life was simple and problems were few and far between. They used to tell us that our biggest worry would be finding ways to use all the spare time created with "labor-saving devices." Well, sorry about that. It didn't work out that way, did it? Most folks today have more to do than they can say grace over, and more problems than they can handle. On top of that, every time we turn on the TV or radio it sounds like the world is coming apart.

It would be easy to get caught up in the whirlwind of negativism that is swarming around us. How should you respond when the challenges are so persistent and so enormous? The answer is to remain faithful to the vision God has given you and the calling He has put upon your life. The Holy Spirit will lead you into the Lord's perfect position. The center of God's will is the safest and most prosperous place God could lead you.

For many years I have had to juggle a lot of different jobs, struggling to keep up with my busy schedule, wearing many different hats. I understand it comes with the territory, of course, and I love my job. I know I am where God has called me to serve. But I won't lie. Nothing prepared me for the medical diagnosis in 2005 that turned my world upside down.

For the longest time I heard nothing but silence. Even so, I felt an overwhelming sense of peace—God wasn't angry with me. He made it clear that my job was not to question His authority. My job was to be faithful to the calling. That is when I understood that the Lord was doing things in and through me as He healed me of this illness that He could not do any other way. I am not through the valley yet, and there are things I still do not understand, but God showed me that He is the One who moves mountains. He is the One who calms the storm, and He is the One who makes life-changing miracles possible. I am learning to cultivate a thankful, joyful spirit according to Isaiah 55:12, which says: "You will go out in joy and be led forth in peace; the mountains and hills will burst into song before you" (NIV).

*Whenever we start feeling sorry for ourselves . . . it is helpful to take a look back at what others have gone through in their walk of faith.*

Whenever we start feeling sorry for ourselves, thinking we are mistreated and put upon, it is helpful to take a look back at what others have gone through in their walk of faith. I am certain this is why we have so many stories of suffering and transformation in the Bible, to show us what it means to be faithful when the world is out of whack, and when everything around you keeps changing.

Take the story of Abraham in the book of Genesis, for example. One day, apparently out of the blue, God comes to a man named Abram in the land of Ur and tells him, "Get out of your country, from your family and from your father's house, to a land that I will show you" (Genesis 12:1). That was quite an order, especially since Abram was already an old man, 75 years of age.

But God wasn't being capricious. He made Abram an astonishing promise:

> I will make you a great nation; I will bless you and make your name great; and you shall be a blessing. I will bless those who bless you, and I will curse him who curses you; and in you all the families of the earth shall be blessed.
>
> *verses 2–3*

What would you do in a situation like that? You have no idea where you are going, you are not a kid anymore so you can't just pick up and leave town, but God has made you a wonderful promise. I hope you would do what Abram did: He packed up everything he owned and hit the road.

Up to this point, we have looked at God's providence and what I call survival grace, which is when we just need to hold

125

on a little bit longer until something breaks. I have also shared how God provides opportunities and encouragement for us until He speaks the word, enabling us to move forward. While we are waiting for this victory, we don't always know how to access the gifts that God has given us. Jesus has the victory ready for us but we don't know how to receive it. We are like a blind man trying to find the door. We are unable to enter the place God has prepared for us until someone shows us the way.

It is at this point that we come into what I referred to in chapter 2 as visionary grace, or being filled with the Holy Spirit (see Ephesians 5:18). It is easy to recognize the danger in the midst of a crisis, but it is often more difficult to recognize the opportunity. In order to see the opportunity in any situation we need to have the greatest sight of all, which is insight. If you have insight and the gift of discernment, you may be able to see what God is up to and how He wants to take you forward.

In Abram's case, God was saying He wanted to do a work in Abram's life that was so radical no one would believe it. This was to be the ultimate transformation of a man, a nation and ultimately the whole world. Talk about transformation! For such a change of directions, Abram would need to reprioritize and reprogram everything he had ever thought or believed. As the apostle Paul expressed it, Abram would need to be transformed by the renewing of his mind. He would need to move away from his own country, his family and everything he had known in his long life. But, by the grace of God, Abram did not quibble or complain. He simply picked up his belongings and obeyed God's command.

## The Mystery of Vision

In some ways Abram's response is similar to what happens when new believers realize they cannot continue the same relationships with their old friends anymore. They have come to faith in Jesus Christ, who has given them a higher calling, and suddenly they understand that they cannot change their altitude without changing their attitude. Those old habits, old ways and old friends will tug at them like an anchor until they fall back into the life Jesus had rescued them from. In the book of Proverbs we are told, "There is a way that seems right to a man, but its end is the way of death" (Proverbs 14:12). To experience new life in Christ, our attitudes about a lot of things have to change, but in today's world that can be a struggle.

In the era of Hollywood, hip-hop and all the sensual stimulation on TV flooding the world with images that can sear the minds and consciences of even the most righteous man or woman, it is next to impossible to leave your country and your kindred behind. You can leave your father's house, and you can break away from certain friends and relations, but if God is trying to renew your mind and take you to another level, you will need to make a conscious decision to change the way you see the world. To do that you need to be filled each day with the Holy Spirit and the Word of God.

In Abram's day, just packing up and leaving town was enough to stop the influence that could have made him an idol worshiper. But with all the profanity and vulgar images that saturate modern culture today, freeing yourself from the influence of the secular world is a much harder proposition. But that is what God demands.

*God is trying to renew your mind and take you to another level.*

God told Abram that if he obeyed His commandments, He would make Abram and his descendants a great nation and a blessing to all mankind. It would be easy enough for us to come up with our own vision of greatness. I am sure you could come up with a picture of what that means to you, but it is much more difficult to live up to God's vision of greatness. Not many can live up to His standards. But what the Lord was saying to Abram was, if you will die to your own agenda, Abram, and take hold of My agenda, My calling and My vision for your life, I will give you a wonderful reward. You will be great in My sight, and you will be blessed as the father of nations.

Now Abram might not have felt so blessed in the midst of his struggles. His life was filled with transition; it was turned upside down many times as he tried to follow God. But God was telling him, I am going to guide you, and I am going to bless you. So long as you remain faithful, you and your descendants will receive all the blessings I have promised you. But to remain faithful, Abram had to be conscious at all times of what God wanted him to become.

Think about that for a moment. Sometimes when you are reading the Bible, God may be guiding your thoughts, leading you in the way that you should go. Without thinking, you may reach down instinctively, placing your finger on a certain passage of Scripture, because God is speaking to you, silently, causing you to underline the words He is speaking to your heart. When God wants to share His vision with you and guide your footsteps, there is often a unique marriage of the minds between you and the Lord. In a sense, it is His will and your will joining together to accomplish His purpose for your life.

Let me give you an illustration of how this happens. When a woman becomes pregnant, she has to be committed to all the changes that this new little life growing inside her body will bring. Before long it is obvious that something very different and very important is taking place inside of her. One of the first signs may be morning sickness, which is disturbing, but it is a good and important process in the baby's development. But any way you look at it, for a period of time the natural order of this mother's world is being turned upside down.

When you have been given a vision of new life in Christ, you cannot continue with your own self-centered notions of what you want to do with your life and what you want to be all by yourself. There is new life growing within you that, any way you look at it, is going to disturb your personal equilibrium. Sometimes you may question what is going on in your life. You may squirm a bit, uncomfortable with the idea that God is taking hold of you and transforming you into a new creation. Other times there is a joy and a sense of enthusiasm that can well up within us in anticipation of doing the Lord's work. But what you are feeling is the living seed of the Word of God that has been planted in your heart.

Something new and wonderful is growing within you and it demands to be fed. Doctors tell us that all the crazy and unusual things women want to eat during pregnancy are actually the body's response to the dramatic changes taking place. The body knows that it needs certain nutrients, both for the mother and the baby, so it triggers certain appetites and cravings to satisfy that need. Now, I am not saying that every craving is a healthy one. Mom, you know you can't have just anything you can think of, right?! But what I am saying is that, just as the life growing inside the mother's body creates new demands that need to be satisfied, the reality of Christ living in your heart causes you to desire the things of the Spirit.

Spiritual vision is a mystery and there are many things about this marvelous process that we do not entirely understand. When God begins to birth a new thing in you He causes you to feel what He feels. You will have concerns for the things that God cares about. Now, there are some people who will pray, "Oh, God, tell me what You want me to do. I need to know." But what they are really saying is, "Oh, God, how about a little peek into the future." Then, if they like what they see, they will be willing to proceed with the calling God has given them. But that is not how it works. God says we must surrender our will to His will. Like Abram, we must be willing to pick up our goods and start marching for the promised land.

But there is something else: Divine revelation only comes after you have committed your way to the Lord. If you're faithful and God continues to bless you on the path you are taking, you will eventually come to your own Canaan land. You will discover your promised land, just as Abram discovered his. God was sending Abram to a specific place, in a particular direction. By the same token, the grace of God in our lives has a definite purpose and direction. He is calling us to a particular destination, which means we are to live Christlike lives through the indwelling of the Holy Spirit and daily immersion in the Word of God.

## The Key to Prosperity

God told Abram He was going to take Abram and his family into a land that flowed with milk and honey. Abram's prosperity was meant to help him fulfill our Lord's vision for his life. Money with a mission can be a problem for unfocused Christians. Said another way: When the freed Israelites did not have Moses to remind them of their calling, they cast a golden calf—a false god. Many Christians in the world's most financially blessed nation are casting idols to Mammon and other gods. Back to Abram, God was placing him in the midst of several nations who should have walked with God and known Him. But they had given themselves over to worshiping false gods. So God decided to replace those nations with a new nation that would be fathered by Abram.

Do you realize that part of the calling you have in this world is to be God's representative in this land? God wants you to exemplify His character, His priorities and His truth in the earth. Your assignment will be in a certain location, on a specific job with a particular organization. But wherever He has ordained to send you, He wants His life and His glory to be represented to the world through you. Before He will give all the details of the location of the assignment, He often has tests so that we will walk with Him in intimacy, allowing Him to transform us into the image of His Son's character.

When God told Abram, "I'm going to bless all nations through you," it was a multiple generational vision. He told

*God wants you to exemplify His character, His priorities and His truth in the earth.*

Abram to get out of the influence of those who were taking him toward darkness. Some of us have been raised in Christian families. Others come from places where God is not honored, and if we were to stay in that environment it would be difficult if not impossible to obey God's call on

our lives. God may not be telling you to get away from your mother and father, but He may be telling you to get away from the codependent relationship you have with them. If you are surrounded by ungodly friends or family, God is saying, "Come out from among them and be separate" (2 Corinthians 6:17).

So where is God taking you? What kind of a place was Canaan? The land of Canaan was named for the fourth son of Noah—Ham (see Genesis 10:6). The Bible tells us that Ham's descendants were under a curse because Ham had looked on his father's nakedness (see Genesis 9:21–23). This was a curse that involved sexuality. The people of Canaan became worshipers of Baal, which involved fertility rites and sexual orgies. The Canaanites occupied the coastlands to the north of Palestine, and were known as merchants and farmers. During their time in Canaan they became powerful and wealthy, buying and selling and doing business with seafaring traders from all over the world. They were powerful people in their day, but their world was about to change.

Abram had been given a vision of the new life God had prepared for him. God ordained a place for Abram and his descendants, and work for them to do. Abram wasn't going to find out all the details of that vision in one huge revelation. God had already told him He would lead him and guide him to the place, and Abram understood that God would tell him what he needed to know when the time was right.

I have seen a very similar process at work in the lives of some of our young people. When Christian young people get out of school these days, they are eager to discover God's will for their lives. As they get on the path to their new career, they have no way of knowing what is going to happen. They have plans and dreams of their own, but they cannot know all the particulars up front about what is going to happen. Yet, God frequently gives them a snapshot of the future possibilities and, if their motives are pure, He plants a certain interest or desire in their hearts that can lead them to their goal. He says, "I will instruct you and teach you in the way you should go; I will guide you with My eye" (Psalm 32:8). The promise of divine guidance is at the very heart of the mystery of vision.

As I was thinking about how to explain this principle, I realized that vision is one of the keys to overcoming stress and anxiety in our lives. Many people, both inside and outside the church, have problems trusting God for healing, for finding a mate or for that much needed financial breakthrough. Most people have problems believing that God has a plan that is uniquely designed for their lives. Consequently, they do not even look for divine guidance, and they get all caught up in trying to do everything for themselves. The real problem is not simply weak faith. They have never really gotten to know God in a deep, personal way. How can you expect to live a stress-free and successful life when you are out of fellowship and trying to figure things out all by yourself?

When we are accustomed to doing everything our own way without pausing to ask for insight and direction, we are going to get exactly what we have asked for, which is not very much. The apostle Paul learned that God's strength was more than enough. He discovered that God's strength is made perfect in weakness. When we place our complete trust in God and His wisdom, His divine strength overflows into our lives and renews our strength so that we are able to mount up on wings like eagles. But He is not going to force us to do it His way. The Lord says, "If you think you can do it better than I can, then go right ahead. I will never forsake you, but I'll be watching to see how your plan works out."

## Three Aspects of Vision

We need to have a sensitive and disciplined spirit to understand this concept. God grants vision to those who are prepared to obey His commandments and follow His wise counsel. But there is another principle that you need to know: Not everyone has the same vision, and the vision that is being fulfilled in someone else's life may have nothing to do with what God has in mind for you. You cannot find what you want, or what God wants for you, in someone else's vision, any more than you can understand their life experience without walking a mile in their shoes. But to broaden the focus a bit, let's take a look at three aspects of the gift of vision.

*You cannot find what you want, or what God wants for you, in someone else's vision.*

First of all, we need to understand that God alone has ultimate vision. Vision is His job description. He sees past, present and future, and the prophet Isaiah tells us that God knows the end from the beginning (see Isaiah 46:9–10). No one else can make that claim.

How many people have any idea what God wants them to be doing in this world? There are some people who will say they are sure of that—we know God wants us to live upright and moral lives—but most folks are not living like they have things all figured out. I am sure there are some who are so attuned to the Word of God that they are living in the center of His will, but I am afraid it is not a very big number. For the rest, if they think they have got a handle on things but cannot figure out how to take the next step, what does that say about their level of understanding?

Jesus said that faith the size of a mustard seed can move mountains, but we do not see a lot of mountain moving these days. We pray, we fast, we command Satan to get behind us, yet the mountains never seem to move. So what is missing? Perhaps God is showing us that we have been trying to turn our own agenda into the will of God. We have taken our own self-created vision and convinced ourselves that this is what God had in mind. But to get back to His agenda, we have got to let go and turn it over to Him. We have to allow God to purify and refine the vision so that we can become a useful instrument in His hands.

Once we receive God's vision for our lives, we are not supposed to plot how things should look according to our own imagination. If we do that, we will find that many times the journey we are on may turn out to be very different from what God had in mind. This is because we have put too much of "us" into the equation and too little of Him.

A second principle is that the vision God gives us may have long-term consequences. As long as we are faithful to the vision and obedient to the calling, the blessing remains. But we can short-circuit the blessing by disobedience. The blessing that God originally shared with Abram was transmitted through him to his son, Isaac, and the generations that would come after him. God had said that Abraham's seed would bless every nation. The blessing to Abram's descendants came through the faithfulness of the father.

When Abram and his family received God's blessings, he was rewarded with long life and prosperity. He was faithful to the vision, and because of that God changed his name from Abram to Abraham and made him the father of nations, just as He had promised. Now, I do not want to give the impression that Abraham was perfect, or that he always listened to God. Abraham made some major blunders in his life, I am sorry to say, and one of the biggest was taking his wife Sarah's maidservant to his bed. Abraham and Sarah were very old and still childless, and Sarah said that since she was barren Abraham should conceive a child with her servant, Hagar. But that was not God's idea, and the consequences of their behavior has haunted the nation of Israel ever since.

God let Abraham know how He felt about that, and told him: What you are doing in your flesh, Abraham, I cannot bless. I only promised to bless you as long as you are in fellowship with Me. But Abraham went even further, choosing to make his illegitimate son, Ishmael, the heir to everything he owned. God had said that in their old age Abraham and Sarah would bear a son who would be the heir, but Ishmael was not Sarah's son. So, clearly, God was not going to extend His promise to Hagar's child.

Does all this sound a little too familiar? We often have some sort of Ishmael running around in our lives, don't we? We have wrongly put our confidence in someone or something that God has not blessed. What I am talking about are the ideas and projects and plans we have conceived on our own that are not of God. As long as Abraham obeyed God's voice and kept His commandments, statutes and laws, God continued to bless him. But when he failed to listen, acted willfully on his own and took a path God had not revealed to him, Abraham paid a very heavy price.

Beware of people with controlling attitudes who act like they want to constantly hear from God for you. Now, don't get me wrong. I do believe there are times when God speaks to us through others, but it is always as the Scripture says, in a "still, small voice." God does not need a megaphone. Most of the time God speaks to us in much more practical ways. He is speaking to us now with extreme clarity through His written Word. He speaks through His ministers and teachers, and He speaks through personal revelation delivered directly to our hearts through daily study and meditation on the Word of God. But I think we need to be a little wary of these well-meaning folks who claim to be taking constant dictation from God. Great balance is needed in this regard because the Scriptures say that in the multitude of counselors there is safety.

Understanding your calling in life often comes at the end of a cycle when God's will and the situation you are dealing with come into alignment. Keeping God's laws and statutes may not seem related to hearing His voice, but clearly this is how God works. I love the verse in Proverbs that says, "Trust in the LORD with all your heart, lean not on your own understanding and in all your ways acknowledge Him, and He shall direct your paths" (3:5–6). When we listen to godly counsel, meditate on the Word and keep His commands, we will know how we should live, and we may well hear the voice of God.

## Finding Your Pathway

Some time ago there was a man who was supposed to be one of the major preachers of our generation. I believed he was blessed with anointing and the grace of God. Along the way, he hit a rough patch in his life with his family. Before long he and his wife got a divorce. I was told that the divorce came because of this man's personal willfulness, but instead of admitting his problems he told the national Christian media that he had not been called to marriage, he was called to ministry.

To his way of thinking, he could just let his wife go her own way, then he would find another woman and get on with his life. In seeking to be led by the Spirit, he actually disobeyed a major principle of the Scriptures. The principle is that the Holy Spirit never directs us contrary to the revealed will of God as in the Scriptures. This preacher was not hearing from heaven. He was walking in the lust of the flesh. Clearly, he had lost the ability to distinguish between the commandments of God and his own fleshly desires, and God was not about to let him prosper in his bad choices.

Some of us are in situations where all the fundamentals in our lives are being challenged. We are feeling distress and maybe a little panic, but we know we need to pause for a moment and evaluate what is happening. You cannot just keep going this way; you need to stop right where you are. Maybe it is your family; you need to get together and work things out. Maybe it is the kids and the way their lives are going. Whatever it is, you have got to saturate that situation with prayer, seek the wisdom of God's Word, and you may also need to seek godly counsel from a Christian friend or pastor. Once you make the commitment to seek God's will and follow Him whatever the cost, God can begin doing a work in your life. We all need to be good stewards over the things we know to be the will of God.

The third principle I want to mention is that faithfulness to the vision can result in a sudden release of blessings in your life. If you have been honest with yourself and with God, a new vision of what direction you need to take may come forth aggressively. You might even have one of those Aha! moments. If you have been living the Word to the best of your ability, renewing your mind and walking with God, you may be surprised to wake up one morning with the knowledge that you have been empowered to walk in the way that you should go. You will have a new sense of God's purpose and direction for your life.

> *Trials and tribulations are simply a backdrop against which the glory of God can be seen.*

Early on, Abram was what you might call a nowhere man, running around trying to find his place in the world. But God gave him a bigger vision. He was told that the entire world would be changed by his life, his marriage and his family. But stop and ask yourself: How would you want to treat your family if you knew that the destiny of your family and your descendants for generations to come would depend on your faithfulness to God today? Would you be content to live for the moment, eaten up with your own selfish desires, or would you want to start bearing fruit for God? I want to let you in on a little secret: The future of your family and loved ones *is* dependent on what you do today.

One way or the other, you will leave a legacy for future generations. I do not know how long Jesus may tarry before He returns, but until that day the way you live your life here on this earth will affect your future and the future of your family, forever. And let me tell you something else: There are people in this community who will never know Jesus Christ, and never experience the joy of heaven, unless they see Jesus in your house, your family and your life. Your trials and tribulations are simply a backdrop against which the glory of God can be seen. So how should that knowledge change the way you live?

When we learn to see our world as God sees it, we will know what to say yes to, what to say no to and how to prioritize our resources. The limitations on our resources can be a real challenge. As the leader of a large suburban church, I have to decide how our resources are used. I am also required to decide which positions on our staff are essential and which are not. That means I have to decide who keeps their job and who doesn't when funds are tight. These are not easy decisions, but it is something I must do.

Just because we are Christians doesn't mean the difficult decisions do not touch our lives. We can be saved and obedient to the will of God and still go through times of hardship and sacrifice. At those moments we simply have to trust that the vision God has imparted to us will help to clarify and purify the path ahead. We read in Proverbs that "the path of the just is like the shining sun, that shines ever brighter unto the perfect day" (Proverbs 4:18). We may not know everything that is about to happen, but we can rely on the counsel of Scripture and the knowledge we have gained to shed light on the road ahead.

Proverbs also says, "Commit your works to the LORD, and your thoughts will be established" (Proverbs 16:3). The

word *established* in this passage means clarified or crystal-
lized. If we commit our works to the Lord, even if we have
to go through hardship or illness or financial stress in the
short term, God will be with us on the journey and lead us
to a better place. We need to turn our cares over to Him so
that our steps will be ordered by the Lord. In other words, in
the moment when you are 100 percent committed to God's
vision, whatever that may require, there will be step-by-step
guidance on the narrow pathway through the hard times into
the safety of His divine purpose for your life.

While you are on the path, there will be times where you
may need to cut back on your plans. Some of your dreams
and big ideas may not be realistic, or they may be premature,
and God is not going to prosper those things. There may be
some decisions we do not want to make, so we feel the pressure. But the Lord knows where we are going. He knows the
end from the beginning. This means that if we continue to
walk in His counsel, God will see to it that we come out at
the right place, at just the right time.

## Finding Your Purpose

Paul is careful to warn new believers that, no matter how
sincere you may be in your commitment to follow in the footsteps of Jesus, the old sin nature is never very far behind. We
all run into that, don't we? For some folks it is like there are
ruts in the road that go to all the old places where you used
to hang out, and you have got to grab hold of the steering
wheel and change directions. The sin nature is there, but we

don't have to accept it. It is easy to remain faithful to God's vision for your life in times of plenty, but it is much more difficult to stay on the pathway when things are changing, or when everything seems to be going wrong.

Following Jesus does not mean we have to be absolutely perfect. We will never be perfect in our own strength. That is more than we can handle, but God has given us a very high standard of righteousness. In the Sermon on the Mount,

> *You will never taste . . . righteousness if you are still skirting around the edges of sin.*

Jesus says, "Be ye therefore perfect, even as your Father which is in heaven is perfect" (Matthew 5:48 KJV). He knows, of course, that we will never be "perfect" in our own strength; nevertheless, He expects us to strive for perfection. That is the goal.

Earlier in the Sermon on the Mount, Jesus says, "Blessed are those who hunger and thirst for righteousness, for they shall be filled" (Matthew 5:6). What a wonderful picture— to be hungry and thirsty for the life that Jesus has called us to live. But I suspect there are some folks who need to hear what I have to say next: You will never taste that kind of righteousness if you are still skirting around the edges of sin and sticking your toe in the pool every once in a while, or if you have decided it is okay to cut loose on Friday and Saturday night, just so long as you are all cleaned up and in your pew on Sunday.

Sin of any kind is an offense to God. It is an affront that calls for honest and sincere repentance and an immediate change of direction. We may slip and fall from time to time, but we have to get right back up and get back on the pathway. That is what it means to hunger and thirst for righteousness.

For business owners, managers or leaders who are responsible for the well-being of their employees, we simply have to exercise good judgment and realize that God cares for our people even more than we do. He knows their needs, and He will provide a way out of trouble. There may be times when our desire to protect our friends, our children or our employees from difficulty and stress may not be the best thing for them. If we truly love those who are closest to us, we have to release them into God's care so He can guide their footsteps even as He is guiding our own.

Some years ago I read a book called *Change or Die*, by Alan Deutschman, which explored the psychology of change. I was fighting a life-and-death struggle at the time, and the book was very helpful to me. Because of the examples the author presented, I was able to deal with the fact that there were some changes I had to make, whether I liked it or not. The book helped me refocus and take a second look at what really mattered in my life.

Deutschman cited several statistics showing that many folks go into a health, financial or career crisis and change their behavior for only ninety days or so, but then they slowly drift back to their former habits, patterns or negative cycles over a six- to twelve-month period. In one example involving people with heart disease who had received the "warning" of a heart attack, a large percentage after a short revival could not make the necessary changes and wound up dying.

The author pointed out three keys to successful change:

1. **Relate:** This is a critical key. There are thousands of personal trainers in the D.C. area, but the one I have been working with the last five years understands my schedule, my training goals and my unique needs (as a cancer survivor).

2. **Repeat:** Follow the mentor's way of doing things until we master them. Matthew 10:24–25 says that when the servant is fully trained, "he will be as his master." Very often the reason a diet or a management system works lies deep within the mundane details.

3. **Reframe:** Once you have truly mastered a certain approach for diet, exercise, language memorization, church planting, etc., you can then add your own flavor.

These three principles are absolutely in sync with biblical discipleship. The concept is laid out in Matthew 10:24–25 and 40–42. On many occasions, I have made a mental decision that a change in my behavior was needed. Unfortunately, I had no wagon on which to hitch my desire for change. First of all, I had no model, no coach. I had no mentor who could lead me in the most direct way to my destiny. Second, I had no proven, personal development system. Every good coach teaches you his system. Finally, once I "own" that system by doing it, I can legitimately personalize the system—and that's when I can put out my shingle: Master/Certified Trainer. In the health world, for example, we need to master P90X or Jenny Craig's weight-loss program before bragging about what we know about fitness.

If you are in a crisis today and God is bringing you through that crisis, you may discover one of these days that God has used this time of stress and uncertainty to bring you to a new level of maturity. In some cases, a period of crisis may be the best gift He could give you. *A gift?* Yes. But what I mean is that in that hour of transition, God was giving you a better and bolder vision so that you could sort out your priorities. He was using stress to turn your attention back to the things that matter most in your life.

As we discern what God wants for each of us, and what His priorities are for our lives, sometimes it is a fairly easy process. We simply listen and learn. But that is not always the case. Sometimes we can only get to the point where God is taking us through trial and error. We may miss the target on occasion. But if we continue faithfully through that time of transition, God will make His will known.

*Crisis is often a way for us to get back on track with God's vision.*

Crisis is often a way for us to get back on track with God's vision. Abram received God's promise that wherever he went he would be blessed. That must have been difficult for Abram to understand at first. God told him that the nations of the earth would be blessed through him. But Abram, to his credit, did not allow the surprising nature of what God was saying to keep him from fulfilling the command he was given. That blessing made Abram a new creation. But I believe God also wants to bless your life, to make you a new creation in Christ and to prepare you to experience success in your life. This is the God who knows everything about you: strengths, weaknesses and limitations. Even though we know all of this, He wants to call forth the champion in you. He is the One who understands how to change our character and transform our world.

He loves you despite your mistakes, and He has a plan for you even in the midst of unimaginable change and discomfort. As long as you continue moving along the pathway toward His goals, God promises to erase your blunders. Your sins are covered by the blood of Christ, who has declared you to be a child of the King. In the inspiring little book *You Were Born for This*, Bruce Wilkerson says, "You are born to do God's work by God's help." He writes that we are born to a life of predictable miracles. No matter what you do in life or how satisfied you may be with the situation you are currently in, you were born to do God's work by God's help. He has created you for a time such as this.

There is a special role in God's plan that only you can fill; there are answers that only you can give. No matter where you are in your life today, and no matter where you will be in a month, a year or a decade from now, I want you to know that you have a purpose and a calling from God. He created you for that purpose. Your task now is to draw closer to Him, to seek His will through the Word and to open your eyes to the vision He has for you, to make you the man or woman He wants you to be.

# ═ 6 ═

# WHAT HAPPENS HERE

## Step Six: Commit Yourself
## to Personal Purity

*I*magine you have heard the TV and radio commercials for Las Vegas that say, "What happens here stays here." The implication, of course, is that when you come to this infamous city of gambling, nightclubbing and late-night escapades, you won't have to worry about what you do getting back to your friends and family back home. It is your little secret, and your private sins will remain private. But there is just one little problem with that line of thinking: It is a lie.

The problem is, *you* would know what happened. It would be locked in your memory and your conscience forever, and if you still have the capacity to feel remorse for your sins, it would continue to grow darker and more disturbing over time. But more to the point, *God* knows what you and I do in private. There are no secret sins, no unrecorded escapades, no time-outs. That is why we need to examine the last and most demanding step in the journey toward transformation: a serious commitment to personal purity.

As I pointed out in chapter 4, the secular world wants nothing to do with Christian morality. For the man or woman addicted to sin, the Christian faith is old-fashioned, repressive, judgmental and confining. Sinners want to be free to indulge in every kind of sin, and they call that "freedom"! But what they are really asking for is not freedom but slavery—slavery to vices and addictions that will only rob them of love, joy, peace, long-suffering, kindness, goodness, faithfulness, gentleness and self-control, which the Bible identifies as the fruits of the Spirit (see Galatians 5:22–23).

Unfortunately, some Christians believe they can dabble in a life contrary to the fruits of the Spirit as well. They have convinced themselves that "freedom in Christ" gives them permission to pursue every sort of pleasure, no matter how dangerous or immoral it may be. They have compromised with the secular values of today's sin-addled culture. And if they start to feel at some point that God is unhappy with what they are doing, they think they can fall back on the old crutch that their sins are forgiven—past, present and future. They are washed in the blood of the Lamb. But do they really believe God is that stupid! Do they really think He will ignore such behavior? The apostle Paul says, "Do not be deceived, God is not mocked; for whatever a man sows, that he will also reap" (Galatians 6:7).

When we come to the end of our rope and realize that we cannot save ourselves—that the old tricks do not work anymore, and that we are sinking deeper and deeper into failure, disappointment and loss—there is only one way back: new life in Christ. The apostle writes, "If anyone is in Christ, he is a new creation; old things have passed away; behold, all things have become new" (2 Corinthians 5:17). There is no other way to find peace and contentment in this life, and that is why a commitment to personal purity is one of the essential steps in transforming your world.

It is time for our churches to deal with the issues that threaten our existence and limit the potential for genuine transformation among our people. I am sad to say that many pastors and teachers refuse to talk about sin and its cure by the blood of Jesus anymore. Too many preachers do not want to talk about the immorality and other dimensions of sin in our churches. They do not want to offend anyone. They do not want to be controversial.

> *I am sad to say that many pastors and teachers refuse to talk about sin anymore.*

Church leaders who have been silenced by this noisy rabble do not want to deal with the wrath of the secular-minded individuals who use the concept of "intolerance" as a weapon against biblical truth and moral responsibility. The church has both an evangelistic role and a prophetic role in the culture. Jesus told His disciples that when the Holy Ghost had come upon them, they would be witnesses. The Greek word for "witness" is the word *martus*, which can also be translated as "martyr." The first apostles were called to literally give up their lives and die for Christ's message and work. We, however, are called to a form of bloodless martyrdom. As we take upon ourselves the call of God—or as some might call it, "the yoke of Christ"—He will give us grace to live His life, do His will and proclaim His message tirelessly (see Matthew 11:28–30). But without getting to the bottom of this issue and returning to God's standard for the family, it would be next to impossible for anyone to achieve the goals set forth in this book. Without a commitment to moral and sexual purity, you will never experience the blessings that God has reserved for those who trust Him and obey His Word.

## Transitional Grace: Making a Personal Covenant With Christ

Sometimes the changes we need to make in our lives can seem overwhelming—too big for any person to achieve on their own. But then, that is what this story is all about. When God wants to do something to change the natural course of events, He does not let the angry mobs stand in His way. He is not limited by the laws of nature. As the Creator of the world and everything in it, He can do the impossible, and He often does. That is why the great stories from the Old Testament are so important for us today. They help us see how God works in the lives of His people.

The story we have been exploring in Joshua 3 is one of the best illustrations I can think of, showing what happens when God's nature and human nature collide. In this story, Joshua is preparing to lead the Israelites into the Promised Land. But there is just one problem, they have to cross the

Jordan River—with millions of men, women and children, and with all their livestock and belongings—while the river is at flood stage.

The situation they faced was similar to what their parents and grandparents faced forty years earlier at the Red Sea. In the book of Exodus we are told, "The children of Israel journeyed from Rameses to Succoth, about six hundred thousand men on foot, besides children. A mixed multitude went up with them also, and flocks and herds—a great deal of livestock" (Exodus 12:37–38). Old Testament scholars estimate that as many as two and a half million people crossed the Red Sea that night with Pharaoh's army in hot pursuit.

The story is powerful because God demonstrated His power and took them across the sea on dry land. Now, forty years later, Moses has reached the end of his leadership and Joshua has been made commander and general over all the people. Somehow they had survived their trials and tribulations; Moses had gone to the mountaintop and brought back the Ten Commandments, but now, as they were nearing the end of their torturous pilgrimage through the wilderness, Joshua had to persuade the people one more time to step out in faith.

Both of these situations are a picture of death, and the people were understandably terrified. How do you persuade the priests leading two million headstrong Israelites to take the first step into the river? But what appeared to be hopeless by man's standards was no challenge for God, who had commanded that the priests bearing the Ark of the Covenant lead the people into the river and cross over to the other side.

Whenever we cross a supernatural boundary and do what
is seemingly impossible, it often requires dying to ourselves.
Joshua never hesitated to obey God's
commands—his faith was unshakable.

*Whenever we cross a supernatural boundary and do what is seemingly impossible, it often requires dying to ourselves.*

For the Israelites, camped with all
their possessions on one side of the
river, marching into the Jordan River
at flood stage must have seemed sui-
cidal. To add to the insanity, the priests
were told to lead the way with the Ark
of the Covenant on their backs. Ob-
viously, they would not have much control as to whether
their feet would slip on the rocks. Once they stepped into
the river, the waters were supposed to part before them, but
was their faith strong enough to risk it? The priests had to
die to any desire for personal safety. They would have no
control over their own destiny. They had to trust that what
Joshua was telling them to do was truly the word of the
Lord. They had to lay their lives on the altar, sacrificing
their own sense of safety, their own ideas about how they
should ford the river and how they would cross over to the
other side.

In the same way, we have to acknowledge before the Lord
that what He requires of us is more responsible and more
sensible than anything we can think up on our own. But you
can be sure of one thing: When God asks you to do something
really big, He won't leave you hanging out there wondering
if it really was His voice you heard. This was a lesson Joshua
had learned years earlier. He knew that God would give him

the confirmation he needed. But when he heard from the Lord, it was time to stand up and be counted.

As we walk out God's vision for our lives, there may be times when He asks us to do things that are risky. In our natural mind we may feel we are going to die if we do what He asks; although at the same time we may fear that we are going to die if we don't.

Over the last several years, the church I pastor has taken a strong stand against same-sex marriage. We do not hate homosexuals, but we believe the Word of God makes it clear that marriage is a sacred covenant between one man and one woman. This is not our opinion; it is God's. But because we refuse to bend our beliefs to satisfy today's politically correct view of homosexuality and same-sex marriage, we are regularly attacked by the other side with vicious slander and even death threats. We are accused of hate speech, but no one seems to notice that all the hate is coming from the other direction. So much so that there are times when I have been concerned for the safety of my family. I have also carried a fatherly concern for the security of all our people. But since God has called us to take a stand for righteousness, we follow His instructions with confidence, despite what it may look like in the natural.

*There are times when I have been concerned for the safety of my family.*

If you think this is just a minor concern or something we could easily ignore, imagine how you would feel if your name and photo were being posted on hate sites all over the Internet. Imagine how you would feel if your picture was published on the front page of the opposition newspapers for weeks on end, and slanderous things were being written about you. We have gone out of our way to be conciliatory and respectful of our opponents, and we have prayed steadfastly to God that our response will never be motivated by hate. Our words and actions are an expression of our belief that the Word of God is true.

As we walk in faith and love, the Lord's name is lifted up. Similar battles are fought by the Body of Christ all over the world. The warfare may be for the heart and soul of a family, a business or a city government. I get numerous letters and emails from around the nation applauding our work. Sometimes these people call upon us to assist them in the work of championing additional causes. Unfortunately, my team and I are only able to encourage them to take up their own crosses, receive their own yokes and enter into their own unique calling with our blessings.

We do not have to be nervous when we are on the side of righteousness. It is those who oppose the will of God who ought to be afraid.


## Restoration and Redemption

In Bible times, the Amorites—inhabitants of Canaan and enemies of the Israelites when God brought the people into the land—were more than nervous. Why? A report on the Israelites was being spread around, saying, "God is with them!" The Israelites had become a danger to anyone who opposed them, and the Amorites were terrified about what was about to happen.

Before the Israelites were allowed to take possession of the land of Canaan, however, God gave Joshua one more command: The people were to make sharp knives and circumcise all the males who had not been circumcised since the flight from Egypt. According to custom, Hebrews circumcised male infants eight days after birth, but they had not followed this custom during their wanderings, which meant that there were men in their thirties, forties and fifties who had never been circumcised. But God told Joshua that no uncircumcised male could enter the Promised Land. Now, you may wonder, why did this matter to God? It mattered because circumcision was a sign of Israel's covenant with God, and He did not want any male crossing into the land who did not bear the mark of the covenant.

The Israelites were no different than we are. When we have missed the mark and made a serious mistake in our lives, we know we have sinned and we expect to come under some sort of judgment or punishment. If we allow any sin or combination of sins to cast a shadow over our lives, we may begin to neglect what we know to be right and true. The devil, who is quick to take advantage when he spots a small weakness, starts whispering in your ear, "Well, you have really done it this time, haven't you?! You messed up so bad, you might as well just wallow in the dirt. You will never pull yourself out of this mess. You are never going to make it to the promised land. You will never achieve your destiny."

If you have heard that voice, know that it is a vicious lie. Satan wants to weaken your resolve and steal you away from the truth that God loves you with an undying love. His love is perfect, everlasting, unconditional and totally unmerited. This, more than anything, is a perfect demonstration of His mercy, which is His unmerited favor. Think of it: When the Israelites rebelled and sinned against God in the wilderness,

*Satan wants to weaken your resolve and steal you away from the truth that God loves you with an undying love.*

they built idols and worshiped them, and committed every sort of sexual sin. But God did not kill the Israelites because they had sinned. He only wanted recognition, repentance, restoration and redemption before they were allowed to enter the Promised Land. The circumcision ceremony was one part of that restoration process. But, by His grace, God provided a way for the nation to be transformed and prepared for their new life.

These words may sound too good to be true, but I have led convicts to Christ. Over the years, some of my members have committed murder, and the memory of that act hangs over their heads and affects their lives forever. There may be things you are ashamed of—things you could never share in polite company. Yet, God can still restore you to fellowship with Him. And He wants to bless the rest of your life.

You may not be able to undo the fact that you had a baby out of wedlock, and you may never be able to forget the fact that, in a moment of desperation and panic, you let them take that baby away from you. You live with that pain and regret every day of your life. You may wonder if God can ever forgive you for what you have done.

Right now, as you read this, God can redeem and restore the rest of your life. You do not have to live out your legacy in terms of what the naysayers have said about you. You do not have to live up to anyone else's idea of what you ought to be doing. God can take you right where you are and fill your life with meaning and purpose. He can fill your heart with song and redeem you from all the grief, doubt, anger and disappointment you have felt for so long. Your purpose is not just about your personal accomplishments. The example you set for the next generations or a Sunday school class may be the greatest contribution you have to offer!

Part of God's judgment on the Israelites for their sin was that they wandered in the wilderness for four long decades. Despite this grim, spiritual prison sentence, their lives counted. Even those who would be left behind because they had been part of the older corrupt generation had a redemptive relationship with God. And if they did nothing more than invest their hopes in the next generation, helping to prepare them for the Promised Land, that would have been a worthy destiny.

God's covenant with the new generation of Israelites was reestablished through the symbolic act of circumcision. That was the price God demanded. Then the new generation replaced the older generation as the covenant people. When those events were finally complete, the men were given time to recuperate, and then the Lord said to Joshua, "This day I have rolled away the reproach of Egypt from you" (Joshua 5:9). And the name of the place where they had camped was changed to Gilgal, which means "rolling."

God rolled away the reproach of Egypt. This expression
has various levels of meaning. Remember, these people had
been captives in Egypt for 430 years and had developed a
slave mentality. Many had come to believe the Egyptians
were all-powerful and superior. Many Israelites had become
so dependent on their slave masters that their masters were
given a godlike status. The Israelites never lacked food while
they were in bondage: The Egyptians fed them and clothed
them. They never had to plan ahead: Every day was the same.
They worked in the kilns and quarries, and did whatever their
slave masters told them to do.

*Our days and our
lives belong to God,
and He rewards each
of us according to
His mercy and grace.*

Do you realize how many people
in our generation have developed an
entitlement mentality? They feel they
are owed something. It has crept into
the whole culture. Some people have
let the government become their god.
They do not want to leave the planta-
tion and earn it for themselves; they want privileges because
they think they are entitled. They are living with a slave
mentality. For folks like this, it may be scary to live without
a government safety net. Other folks have faithfully served a
company most of their adult lives only to be told the company
cannot give them the pension they had been promised. Others of us remember an America in which making money was
much easier than it is today. No matter how we have arrived
at this entitlement mindset, we have begun to expect life to
give us profits, results and security that it can no longer offer.
Welcome to freedom!

I will never forget when my wife had to stop working for health reasons. I felt like Job. Soon after I was raised up from my bed of affliction, my wife contracted blood cancer (multiple myeloma) and had to stop working. After prayer and thanksgiving, a clear plan came to me about how to reclaim my career and finances. Time will not allow me to give you a blow-by-blow testimony. It is sufficient to say that if my life were a movie, there would be too many subplots and mini-crises to count. But we win with God no matter how "the odds" seem stacked against us.

The beautiful thing about serving God is that it does not matter who is in power or who thinks they are entitled to your money or your property or any of the things you have earned for yourself. Our days and our lives belong to God, and He rewards each of us according to His mercy and grace. There may be racism or classism or sexism or all kinds of "isms" out there, and we can deal with that. But you and I need to understand that we have a one-on-one personal relationship with the Creator of the universe. He is the One who supplies our needs, and He is the only authority to whom we are ultimately responsible. He is above all, and He is the keeper of our souls.

## Taking the Next Step

Just as God removed the reproach of the Israelites, He can free our hearts from the stain of selfishness, bitterness and thoughtlessness that are at the root of every sin. He is the One who holds the future and the One we trust to show us the way ahead. But the slave mentality is not just a way of thinking, it becomes a way of life that can take root in your soul if you do not have your eyes fixed on Jesus. You can start to feel worthless, that you will always be a second-class citizen. After years of beating their heads against the wall, some folks subtlely start to believe they have no right to the promises of God.

"Rolling away" the reproach means a new beginning! The words of Joshua 5:10–11 are instructive:

> And the children of Israel encamped in Gilgal, and kept the passover on the fourteenth day of the month at even in the plains of Jericho. And they did eat of the old corn of the land on the morrow after the passover, unleavened cakes, and parched corn in the selfsame day.
>
> *KJV*

Israel celebrated the Passover. Why did they do this? Because God wanted the new generation to remember that they had been delivered from death, just as their parents and grandparents had been delivered from Pharaoh. The angel of death had slaughtered the firstborn sons of the Egyptians and anyone else who failed to apply the blood of a lamb to their doorposts.

As a sign of their covenant with God, Israel's firstborn had been spared. But as Joshua led this new generation into the land of destiny, they needed to remember the old places of death and destruction and the plagues that had crushed the spirit of their Egyptian masters. By the same token, Jehovah wants us to remember that He has brought us out of our addiction to sin. And He wants us to remember that He is the One who goes before us to defeat every foe. The lost job, the foreclosure, the economic decline and the bankruptcy may come to everyone else's house, but when the angel of death passes over your house, it is not because of your righteousness. It is because of the righteousness of a holy and all-knowing, loving God who cares for you.

When the older generation of Israelites first fled from Egypt and crossed safely over the Red Sea, they were rejoicing, celebrating the blessings of an all-powerful God. Scripture says that as they went, there was not one feeble person among them (see Psalm 105:37). They were healed of all their ailments and diseases before they crossed the Red Sea. Furthermore, they had received a financial contribution from the Egyptians, who showered them with gold and treasures of every kind before they departed.

God had protected them and spared their families from the death of firstborns. So they had family wholeness. Finally they were leaving the land of paganism and immorality for a new land with freedom of access to Jehovah God. At long last they could enjoy the freedom of worship. For the new generation led by Joshua, the celebration of Passover was more than just a symbolic reminder that God had released them from slavery. To this day observant Jews celebrate Passover as a reminder of how God provided for the Israelites on the day of their release from bondage. But it was a reminder to the Israelites that they needed to remain faithful and obedient to the Lord their God.

## It Is for Freedom That Christ Has Set Us Free (Galatians 5:1)

Despite the many reasons for God's people to celebrate their deliverance from Egypt, they were afraid to advance much farther. Moses said, "You have reached the hill country of the Amorites, which the LORD our God is giving us. . . . Go up and take possession of it as the LORD, the God of your fathers, told you. Do not be afraid; do not be discouraged" (Deuteronomy 1:20–21 NIV1984). He was ready to march, but the people said, "Let us send men ahead to spy out the land for us and bring back a report about the route we are to take and the towns we will come to" (verse 22).

At that point, Moses agreed to send twelve men into the land of the Amorites as spies. Perhaps this will help you understand why the older generation was not allowed to enter the Promised Land. But what the people were actually saying, was, "Okay, we hear you, Moses. You said God is with us, but we are not going to believe it unless you allow us to send in some spies." Then, when the spies came back and confirmed that the Lord was giving them a land flowing with milk and honey, they still did not believe that God would live up to His promises, because the spies reported giants in the land.

In Joshua 5, we are told that on the day after they celebrated Passover, the manna that had kept them alive for so long suddenly stopped. This was the bread the Lord had provided, the Israelites' survival grace, and the minute they reached the place where they could survive on their own, the manna stopped.

There is a season when God reaches down and, through His unmerited favor, lifts us out of the hole we have dug for ourselves. Perhaps you have even experienced this in financial matters, where you did not know how you would manage to keep body and soul together, but somehow God's protection was at work and you came through the worst of it. He gave you a measure of His grace. But after this season has passed, He presents us with another view of how His grace works. He gives us insight as to how to go forward, a vision of the direction we should take, but at some point the manna stops and you have to strike out for the promised land in faith.

Many times God points the way ahead through a Scripture that leaps off the page, through insight, through a dream or through a strong sense of His leading, and that vision allows you to move into the blessing God has ordained for you. Very often in the middle of a problem, when you're crying out for deliverance, God will begin to guide your thoughts, showing you how to renew your mind, change your way of thinking or alter how you have been doing things. Some folks will never do a quality "postmortem" on their bad decisions until they hit the brick wall of failure, but reflection can be a valuable part of the learning process as well. There is something about messing up—about reaching the point of no escape—that can make you take stock of your life and realize that something needs to change.

> *Many times God points the way ahead through a Scripture that leaps off the page, through insight, through a dream or through a strong sense of His leading.*

When God stopped the blessing of food that He had been dropping down from heaven, this was not a curse. The manna ceased because the Israelites had arrived at their destination and no longer needed that blessing. They were entering the land of Canaan, which was an agriculturally based economy with more than enough to feed all the people. There was such wealth and abundance, they could trade their produce with other nations. Although they had been slaves for 430 years, God put them in a position where they could become rich and successful, so long as they continued to look to Him for their strength.

## Making the Hard Choices

I believe God wants us to be strong and prosperous. He wants us to rise above our challenges, but we only overcome adversity, heartache and fear when we put God first in our lives. He ought to be Lord of our careers, our dreams and even our families and friends. Jesus said that anyone who desires to follow Him will have to make some hard choices. He said that households may be divided over whom they will serve: "Father will be divided against son and son against father, mother against daughter and daughter against mother, mother-in-law against her daughter-in-law and daughter-in-law against her mother-in-law" (Luke 12:53). There will be division, Jesus said, for no other reason than whether or not a person is willing to lay aside every thought, every habit and every temptation that is not of God.

Now that you know what God expects of you, I want to ask, whom will you serve? After the Israelites had crossed over the River Jordan into Canaan, and after God had miraculously driven the Amorites and six other nations out of the land, many of the people were in danger of sliding back into the old ways, worshiping strange gods and participating in every kind of sin. So Joshua called the people together and gave them a fateful challenge: "Choose for yourselves this day whom you will serve, whether the gods which your fathers served that were on the other side of the River, or the gods of the Amorites, in whose land you dwell." He said it was their decision to make. You might say they had freedom of religion in that day, too. Joshua was not going to force them to make the right choice, but he said, "As for me and my house, we will serve the LORD" (Joshua 24:15).

Today, in the second decade of the 21st century, we are at a crossroads in this country, and we are being asked to choose whom we will serve. Whose report are we going to believe about our lives and the life of the church? As 21st-century Christians, are we or are we not called to be a prophetic voice to the nations? Are we or are we not called to transform the lives of the people who live around us? Are we or are we not called to take the supernatural message of God's healing power and the gifts of the Holy Spirit to this generation?

God issues us this challenge. It is not my challenge. God has put us at the crossroads and shown us a vision of the two ways we can go. If the church of Jesus Christ is to make a difference in today's world, then each of us as individuals will have to make a difference in our world. In some cases that will mean making a clean break with some of your old friends. You may have to part ways with certain members of your own family who prefer to worship, as it were, the gods of the Amorites.

Or maybe you need to take an even greater risk, breaking the pattern of unbelief in your family tree in order to burst through the holding pattern that seems to have settled down on your life. So this is an important question. It is hanging there before you, and you have got to answer it: Are you going to believe the report of the Lord and follow Him? Or are you going to take sides with today's sin-soaked secular culture that has rejected the true witness of God?

Some of you reading this book today may need to break the cycle of addiction in your family. Maybe you need to stop the long stream of broken homes that has come down through the generations to you. Maybe you need to change your attitude about how you can experience the blessings of heaven and put an end to the cycle of poverty that has crushed the spirit of your family for generations. So let me ask you one more time: Whose report are you going to believe?

Whoever you are and wherever you may be, the world does not want you to truly succeed. God wants the very best for you; He wants you to soar with wings like eagles. But the world would be much happier if you settled for something less; it would have you just continue to stumble along, dependent on the system, living in darkness. But God is telling you it is time to stop seeing yourself as a failure and start seeing that He has given you everything you need to succeed.

You may be sitting in a place of authority in this world, but until you have reached out to God and started following Him each day, you are going nowhere. Your bank accounts may be full of this world's treasures, but all that gold will do absolutely nothing for you when you stand before God and He calls for an accounting of how you have lived your life.

If you want to experience true success, both in this world and the next, you will never get there by following the self-serving politicians and bureaucrats who are doing everything they can to keep you in bondage. Why are you letting darkness and unrighteousness rule your life? And why are we allowing so much corruption and greed to continue in our cities and towns?

> *God wants the very best for you; He wants you to soar with wings like eagles. But the world would be much happier if you settled for something less.*

I believe that God has called His church to take back our nations for Christ. We can be the answer to the problems that plague us today. God's people need to rise up in this hour and accept His gift of grace. But we will need to catch the vision before we can walk in His will. We need to get the revelation for His will for our lives, both corporately and personally. Some folks do not pay the price because they do not know what is expected. Others do not know that now is the day of salvation. They are paralyzed by fear so they are not going to make the hard choices, either at home or in the workplace, to see real transformation take place. Instead, they are going to allow unredeemed schoolteachers and college professors to strip away the reverence from their children. They allow the media, the politicians and the hustlers of every sort to trivialize and desecrate the things of God. Wisdom is necessary as we take our personal faith stand. But courage is also needed.

Those who serve the gods of the Amorites, Hittites, Girgashites, Cancannites, Perizzites, Hivites, Jebusites—which is to say, the gods of their own belly, their sinful lusts and their worldly appetites—are not going to take a stand for righteousness. They are going to keep on putting their trust in leaders who serve their own bellies and whose aim and purpose is to accumulate power and wealth for themselves, and to corrupt the system. These people are not going to cross over into the promised land. But how long will you and I go along with such people? Yes, they seem to have all the power, and they speak with high and lofty words, but their actions leave no doubt that they despise our beliefs and Christian values.

God is calling His church to shake off the yoke of slavery. He wants us to understand that men and women in the household of faith can make a difference in this generation if we are truly willing to make the hard choices. The secular world has dictated how we live, how we eat and drink, how we vote and even how we think, for generations now. That is long enough, and God is telling us it is time to stand up and say, "No more!" We have the power and the godly authority to take the land, but to do that we will need to respond to Joshua's challenge: Choose this day whom you will serve.

## On Holy Ground

Several years ago, during a trip to England, a well-known preacher called me forward during a church service and placed offering buckets over my head. He had a personal prayer for me, and he felt led to pray that I was not going to have financial problems any longer, and my ministry was not going to lack for money ever again. After the service, he encouraged me to believe God and I would see major changes in just ninety days. Of course I loved what he said that night, and I was so

*God is telling us it is time to stand up and say, "No more!"*

excited at the end of ninety days, that I expected the heavens to open up at any moment. However, I had the same experience the Israelites had when they crossed over the Jordan—the manna stopped.

Almost overnight our funds dried up and the ministry went into the worst financial downturn we had ever experienced. The church began to go through struggles exactly opposite of what that pastor had declared. In this "Death Valley" of our ministry, I lost over one thousand members and several million dollars of ministry income. Personally, Vivian and I had received hospital bills for up to $100,000 at a time. But then, as I came to understand and apply the principles of transformation that I have shared in these pages, everything began to change.

First, I had to rediscover the power of humility in my life. This was taking things to a different level. Second, I came to see that God's power and authority were more than enough for me, but they could only come forth when I admitted my own weakness and committed my way to His leadership and guidance. This taught me to trust God more than ever. Third, I came to see Christ's commandment to love my neighbor as

I love myself in a whole new way, and as I did that, my desire to reach out and share the love of God with others began to blossom. Fourth, as I thought about the challenges I had faced in my own life, I understood that Christ has already given us the victory. We are more than conquerors when we place our lives in His loving hands.

As I began to apply each of those principles, I accepted the fact that there were many things I needed to learn. My wife, Vivian, and I had to endure many unsettling changes before we entered the promised land in our personal lives, but we were willing to accept those changes because we could see that God was shaping our destiny. That was the fifth principle, and a very important turning point in my ministry.

Finally, the sixth principle was seeing how intensely God cares about personal holiness and sanctification in our lives. Titus 3:10 declares that the grace of God teaches us not to sin. God, in His goodness, weans us off of sin.

Sometimes our God breaks the chains of addiction suddenly and completely. Other problems, habits and family sin patterns may take years to beat. They may require great diligence and hard work to overcome. But through it all I have found that by His grace our God awakens a deep desire for personal purity as we walk with Him. Then thoughts, words and deeds are probed with the loving but persistent pressure of the Holy Spirit in that area of my life. The Lord challenges us to right relationships, break habits, correct attitudes and take decisive action of some kind.

David was often in this postion in his journey toward personal holiness. He finally came to a point where he prayed that God would help him sort out his troubling thoughts and enable him to progress in his journey toward holiness (see Psalm 139). For me, I began to understand how much God hates sin and how He withholds His favor from those who consistently compromise with self-indulgence. I knew there were some in the church who were trying to have it both ways. I had even heard certain Christian leaders downplaying the dangers of sin. Others preach that Christians never have to repent of sin after they are saved—directly contradicting 1 John 1:7–8. Some people only harp on sexual sins. Sexual sins are not the most significant sins in the Scriptures. They are binding and addictive, though. The Scriptures are clear that we are to "flee sexual immorality." This is huge in the age of sexual promiscuity and excess in which we live. Nonetheless, pride, greed and the long list of the works of the flesh in Galatians 5 can be snares or traps for any of us.

Amazingly, I discovered that the Lord wanted me to walk with Him in a progressive journey of holiness so that He could cleanse my thoughts and the huge arena of motives. In some ways, the areas of manipulation, control and deceitful leadership can be the most hurtful sins within the Body of Christ. It is sufficient to say that relearning to live with "an open hand" and "an open book" were important lessons for me. In addition, attempting to serve others and use my resources to bless and promote the Lord's agenda instead of my own became more important to me than at any other point in my life.

As I began to apply those principles in my life and ministry, things began to change. Within a matter of weeks we were receiving gifts and donations in amounts we had never seen before. Several hundred thousand dollars came in, completely unexpectedly. Suddenly we were subduing a new territory, and we were going to have to learn how to navigate in a new dimension of finance, not only with tithes and offerings but with an outpouring of God's incredible bounty. God wanted us to know that we would gather from whatever source He made available to meet our needs.

That was a miracle, but the same kinds of miracles are happening today. By the time this book is released, we will have totally turned our financial picture around. In addition, our ministry is headed in a new direction. In the bank of heaven, God has all the resources we will never need, and He has given us the seed money. The Lord may provide for His vision in our lives through secular hands. Philippians 2:13 reveals a powerful aspect of grace: "For it is God who works in you to will and to act in order to fulfill his good purpose" (NIV). There are some folks reading this book who need to learn how to operate in a new kind of finance. Instead of putting on the brakes when things are going downward, you may need to step on the accelerator and move forward into God's purpose and plan for your life. We must learn how to discern His timing.

There is another important lesson in Joshua's story that I think we need to hear at this point. In Joshua 5:13–14, Joshua comes face-to-face with an armed man he does not recognize. Many biblical scholars believe this may have been an appearance of Jesus Christ in the Old Testament. The passage says, "When Joshua was by Jericho, that he lifted his eyes and looked, and behold, a Man stood opposite him with His sword drawn in His hand. And Joshua went to Him and said to Him, 'Are You for us or for our adversaries?'"

Joshua realized this was no ordinary man. If this were an ordinary man, Joshua, who was one of the mighty warriors of Israel, would not have responded in this way. But seeing a man of war standing before him, Joshua wanted to know if this man bearing

> *Relearning to live with "an open hand" and "an open book" were important lessons for me.*

a sword was on Israel's side. The answer took Joshua by surprise: "No, but as Commander of the army of the LORD I have now come" (Joshua 5:13–14). Hearing those words, Joshua did what any rational man would do. He fell on his face and worshiped, and then asked, "What does my Lord say to His servant?"

Joshua was no fool. If God sent the commander of His army to meet him, Joshua wanted to make it perfectly clear that he was all ears. He basically said, "Just tell me what you want and I am your man." There was only one agenda Joshua truly cared about, God's agenda, and that is why stories like this are so important for us to study. This is how you operate in the area of transitional grace. Please remember that transitional grace is nothing more than cutting a personal covenant with God so that He can bring us into His destiny for us. This is where we learn how to work with the transforming grace that God is offering us today. This is where we receive instruction on how things operate in the kingdom of God. It is not about us; it is not about our self-centered dreams. It is about the transforming vision that God is bringing forth in each of us.

As soon as Joshua made it clear to the angel of the Lord that he was fully on board with His agenda, the armed warrior said, "Take your sandal off your foot, for the place where you stand is holy" (Joshua 5:15). And what do you think happened next? The passage continues, "And Joshua did so." There was no hesitation. He did not ask for clarification or more time, and he did not ask for any explanation. Confronted by the will and authority of God, he did as he was told.

This is very similar to what happened to Moses at the burning bush. Moses had fled from the wrath of Pharaoh and was wandering around in the wilderness. He had not yet been called to deliver the Israelites from Egypt at that point, but God appeared to him in a burning bush and told him, "Take your sandals off your feet, for the place where you stand is holy ground" (Exodus 3:5). Like Joshua, Moses did not hesitate. He did not even look back at the bush. He immediately turned his eyes away and removed his sandals. For both these men who were called by God to lead the people of God, removing their shoes was an act of worship. They were entering into a covenant relationship with Him.

> *I pray that you are prepared to stop whatever you have been doing that is displeasing to God.*

As one preacher said, taking off their shoes was a way of letting go of their egos, their sense of pride. When we put our own interests ahead of God's interests, this preacher said, we are just trying to "ease God out"—E.G.O. There are too many Christians, including a lot of Christian leaders, who think they can get to their own promised land in their own strength. But Moses and Joshua knew better. Confronted by the holiness of God, they fell to the ground and worshiped the King of kings and Lord of lords.

As you go forward in your own walk of faith, I pray that you are prepared to stop whatever you have been doing that is displeasing to God and acknowledge your debt of gratitude and worship to the King of kings. I hope you have already begun the process of eliminating every thought, habit and temptation from your life that can prevent you from experiencing true and lasting transformation.

The message of this world is that what happens here is just your little secret; no one needs to know. But in God's world, that way of thinking will not fly. God has a purpose for your life. He loves you with an everlasting love and wants to demonstrate His saving grace in your life. But you will need to demonstrate by your behavior each day and your faithfulness to His Word your willingness to live by His rules.

The message of this book is that God wants you to be a demonstration project of His love to everyone around you; but before He can take you to the next level, He needs to know that there are no false gods in your closet, and no empty promises competing for your attention. It is my sincere hope that the principles we have discussed in these pages will help you to become the person you were born to be.

# AFTERWORD

*The Person You Were Born to Be*

ow do you find favor with God? When the angel came to Mary, the mother of Jesus, he gave her some remarkable news: "Rejoice, highly favored one, the Lord is with you; blessed are you among women!" (Luke 1:28). As you can imagine, the sudden appearance of the angel startled Mary—I am sure it would startle anyone—but Gabriel said, "Do not be afraid, Mary, for you have found favor with God" (verse 30).

Why was Mary chosen to bear the Son of God? What had she done to deserve that honor? We know Mary was descended from the line of David, which was a fulfillment of prophecy. And we know that Mary was faithful to God, obedient to her family and devout in her religious devotion. History tells us that she was barely a teenager, so I can deduce that a pure heart is our biggest asset. But what God saw in Mary, I would suggest, was not simply her sincere faith but her willingness to accept the instructions of the angel Gabriel without hesitation.

Once she understood that she had been chosen to become the mother of the Son of God, Israel's Messiah, she said simply, "Behold the maidservant of the Lord! Let it be to me according to your word" (Luke 1:38). That was not an easy decision because Mary was not married. She must have known she would be accused of sin and tormented by her neighbors, but Mary never questioned the role she was given.

> *God reserves His favor for those who are obedient to Him and are available to do His will.*

This was the task she was born to fulfill, and she rejoiced in it.

As we look back briefly at the six principles discussed in this book—humility, trust, love, faithfulness, endurance and purity—I would like to emphasize why each is an essential step in the journey toward transformation and renewal. Along the way I also want to emphasize the importance of obedience to the Word of God. For believers, there is no greater honor that knowing we have found favor with God, but it is important to understand that God reserves His favor for those who are obedient to Him and are available to do His will.

God has a plan for every one of us if we are truly available. He wants you to experience happiness, success and joy in your life, and He wants you to feel the full impact of His love. But as I pointed out in chapter 1, in order to have a meaningful relationship with Him, you and I need to have a humble and willing spirit. This means that we must be in a place where He can reach us. We need to be near enough to feel His presence—real personal intimacy. We need to be in the Word, reading our Bibles on a regular basis, so He can speak to us in that still small voice and help us deal with our issues and concerns.

You and I need to show reverence and respect for the Lord, but we never need to be afraid in His presence if we are walking daily in the Word. Scripture tells us that if we come to Him openly and honestly, He hears our prayers and blesses us according to our needs. But just as important, we need to understand that we will need to resolve the personal issues, private sins, bad habits, bitterness, anger and any other bad fruit in our lives. We do not want anything to block the full measure of His blessing.

As I suggested earlier, you may need to empty your spiritual pockets of the things you have been holding back. Because God cannot look upon sin, repentance and confession are the essential first steps to cleaning out the attic and starting your relationship with Him on the right foot. Above all, you and I must recognize Jesus Christ as our Savior and Lord. After salvation, we must be willing to make the changes in our attitudes, language and lifestyles that can create barriers between us and God.

Change is not easy at first. Change will feel awkward, but you will be surprised what a huge impact this act of humility and openness before God will have upon your daily life, your happiness and your future success. Opening yourself up to His love, asking for forgiveness and consciously forgiving those who have wronged you in the past is one of the most liberating and healing things you and I will ever do. As Peter writes, "Therefore humble yourselves under the mighty hand of God, that He may exalt you in due time, casting all your care upon Him, for He cares for you" (1 Peter 5:6–7). This is such an important step on the journey toward your destiny as a child of God.

## A Pathway to Blessing

As we saw in chapter 2, our relationship with Christ is a two-way street. Throughout the Scriptures, we see that God is gracious, merciful and worthy of praise. He is faithful and true and always trustworthy. He is someone we can trust, but God wants to know that you and I can be trusted, too—trusted to stretch ourselves and rely on His grace, trusted to do His will. It is one thing to pray every day and show up in church on Sunday, but it is something else to be someone God can count on every day of the week and in every situation.

As I mentioned previously, 2 Chronicles 16:9 makes an amazing statement: "For the eyes of the Lord run to and fro throughout the whole earth, to show Himself strong on behalf of those whose heart is loyal to Him." What an incredible thought! God is looking for loyal, dedicated, obedient men and women to bless. He has known you from your mother's womb and He wants to pour out His blessings on you. But will you be able to receive such a blessing? Are you available to Him? To experience the favor of God in your life you need to be someone He can trust.

In chapter 3, we looked at the broad concept of love and the importance of the family. Our homes should have a healing presence. Unfortunately, some of us have experienced a father wound that has prevented us from being emotionally whole.

I consider myself very fortunate to have grown up in a stable and loving home with both parents and my brother, and I often feel sadness for those who have not been quite so blessed. Faithfulness to God will become easier and easier as we learn to live in His ecosystem.

> *It is one thing to pray every day and show up in church on Sunday, but it is something else to be someone God can count on every day of the week and in every situation.*

Despite the discomfort we often feel, God's love is unchanging and His Word is unfailing. When we commit our way to the Lord and trust in Him, the psalmist tells us the Lord will intervene in our situation and grant us advantages in the midst of adversity (see Psalm 37:5). The concept of a love ecosystem has to do with learning how to receive God's mercy and grace personally. Next we learn the love walk in our homes. Third, our churches need to follow God's blueprints so that love and grace permeate our world. Jesus said in John 13:35 that they will know you are My disciples by your love.

As a minister, I understand Christ's words in the Sermon on the Mount: "Love your enemies, bless them that curse you, do good to them that hate you, and pray for them which despitefully use you, and persecute you" (Matthew 5:44 KJV).

Believe me, I know how hard that can be. But this is the essence of God's love. God calls us to be emissaries of His love, but that doesn't mean we have to lie down and let those who do not share our values roll over us.

The ability to persevere in the face of adversity is an important trait of believers in Jesus Christ, and this is at the heart of our discussion in chapter 4. Endurance is one of the six steps to gaining control over your destiny and a virtue that is essential in every important endeavor, whether it is on the playing field, the classroom, the workplace or the home. There will be times in life when we are tempted to quit and give up. Sometimes the days are too long, the job is too hard, the people around us are too unkind and the rewards are too slow in coming. But victory is never easy when the struggle really matters.

When you find yourself surrounded by barbarians who seem determined to make your life miserable, I invite you to try this simple response: Pray for them. You do not need to tell them what you are doing, just pray for them, privately, and do your best to forgive them regardless of the provocation. You will be surprised and amazed at the change this can make in your life. Once you hand the problem over to God, He begins the process of freeing you of the discomfort and pain you may be feeling, and the change taking place within you will have an impact on the problems you are facing. Jesus knew we would have to go through hard times in this life, and that is why He tells us, "In the world you will have tribulation; but be of good cheer, I have overcome the world" (John 16:33).

# Living With Anticipation

In chapter 5 we took the concept of endurance a step further, looking at the importance of remaining faithful in the midst of change. We also looked at an amazing coping mechanism God often grants to His children when we have important decisions to make: the mystery of vision. This is something the non-Christian world has a hard time understanding, that our faith is not simply a bunch of hymns and prayers and hollow rhetoric on Sunday mornings but a vibrant and dynamic interaction with the God of the universe. What makes the Christian life so powerful and exciting is that God answers our prayers and intervenes on our behalf.

At the writing of this book, many Christians believe our nation is about to experience divine judgment. It is true that God chastens those He loves (see Hebrews 12:6). Fortunately for us, our Lord has mastered the ability to "keep us" as individuals even while He is spanking a nation. At this time in our nation's history, it would be easy to become depressed and angry about what is happening all around us. The economy is apparently broken, millions of Americans are out of work, millions more have lost their homes and investments and the cost of living has gone through the roof. On top of all that, our streets are no longer safe, our kids are being lured by fads, fashions and dangerous behaviors that can only hurt them and the country is so morally, spiritually and politically divided there seems to be no way of turning things around.

In times like these we can take heart in the knowledge that God hears our prayers. It is reassuring to know that, no matter how bad the situation may be and no matter how deep the pit we have fallen into, there is always a way out. This is the advantage we have as believers in Jesus Christ, the knowledge that we are never alone and even on the darkest days, He is there with us. One of the most encouraging Bible verses I know reminds us of Christ's promise: "I will never leave you nor forsake you," then adds, "The LORD is my helper; I will not fear. What can man do to me?" (Hebrews 13:5–6).

It is because the God that offers these promises is dependable that we can stand boldly during uncertain times. We know there will be struggles along the way, and it still takes courage to get up every morning and do all the things we have to do. It takes determination and self-sacrifice now and then just to keep putting one foot in front of the other, but we do it because we know that, as the apostle reminds us, "I can do all things through Christ who strengthens me" (Philippians 4:13).

> *No matter how bad the situation may be and no matter how deep the pit we have fallen into, there is always a way out.*

The final admonition of this work, then, and the one that brings all the others together, is the importance of personal moral purity. This is an area the outside world would prefer to ignore. The mainstream culture has done everything possible to convince us there should be no limits on human sexuality. Beyond sexuality, there is a realm of purity in our thoughts, words and deeds that may be captured. The kind of inner purity that causes us to turn the other check while praying for the salvation of our persecutors.

We must learn how to walk in the Spirit. I believe the internal alarm that sociologist James Q. Wilson refers to as "the moral sense" is telling us there are barriers we should not cross, and crossing them only leads to unhappiness and pain. There are also positive spiritual alarms that expose us to new faith opportunities. Isaiah prophesied, "Ye shall go out with joy and be led forth with peace" (Isaiah 55:12 KJV). To achieve the destiny that God has planned for each of us, we need to resist the pressures, temptations and threats the secular society has used to try to break the spirit of believers. We need to immerse ourselves in prayer to withstand the assault, but as I discovered in my own life, it is worth the effort and it pays eternal rewards.

Are you ready to become the person you were born to be? I trust you are, and that is why you have worked your way through these pages. I hope you understand that God has not gone away, He is not silent and He is your defender and friend. If you truly want to move ahead to the next step, to put the past behind you and move on to the destiny that God has in store for you, I hope you will think about the significance of these six areas of concern—humility, trust, love, faithfulness, endurance and purity—and the role that each of them can play in your life.

In closing, let me ask once again, do you want to walk with the God of love? Do you want to become someone God can trust? Are you willing to be that kind of person? I hope your answer will be yes, and that you are ready to experience the joy and the adventure of new life in Christ. My sincere hope is that when God casts His eyes your way, He will see that your heart is loyal to Him, and the blessings of heaven will begin to flow into your life as never before. You were born for more than this world can offer, so I want to encourage you to step forth boldly and claim your destiny as a child of the King.

Harry R. Jackson Jr. is senior pastor of Hope Christian Church, a 3,000-member congregation just outside the nation's capital. He is also the host of the nationally syndicated talk show *The Harry Jackson Show*, heard daily on American Family Radio and several other radio networks within the U.S. Having earned an MBA from Harvard, Bishop Jackson approaches ministry from a unique perspective. His writing is featured in periodicals such as the *Washington Post*, the *New York Times*, *Charisma*, *Ministry Today* and the *Christian Post*. Bishop Jackson has appeared on CNN, *CBS Evening News*, MSNBC, BET, *The O'Reilly Factor* on FOX and the Christian networks CBN and TBN. His previous books include *In-laws, Outlaws and the Functional Family*; *The Warrior's Heart*; *The Way of the Warrior*; the Gold Medallion Award–nominated *High Impact African-American Churches*; *Personal Faith, Public Policy* and *The Truth in Black and White*.

Bishop Jackson is also the founder and president of High Impact Leadership Coalition, which exists to protect the moral compass of America and be an agent of healing to our nation by educating and empowering churches and community and political leaders. The energy of this organization and the grassroots mobilization produced by it have impacted government officials locally, in multiple states and in the federal government. Visit www.thetruthinblackandwhite.com for more information.

Bishop Jackson has been recognized as a leader of leaders. He is in demand to minister both nationally and internationally. He has recently formed the International Communion of Evangelical Churches, which oversees more than 1,200 churches around the world. He and his wife, Vivian,* have two daughters and live in Silver Spring, Maryland. For more information, visit www.thehopeconnection.org.

---

* Although her given first name is Vivian, for most of her life Bishop Jackson's wife has been known by her middle name, Michele. Recently, while battling—and overcoming—multiple myeloma, she decided to reclaim Vivian, which means "alive" or "living."